# BODYGUARD

## THE REAL STORY

### INSIDE THE SECRETIVE WORLD OF
### ARMED POLICE & CLOSE PROTECTION

**JONATHAN LEVI AND
EMMA FRENCH**

First published in the UK by John Blake Publishing
An imprint of The Zaffre Publishing Group
A Bonnier Books UK company
4th Floor, Victoria House
Bloomsbury Square,
London, WC1B 4DA
England

Owned by Bonnier Books
Sveavägen 56, Stockholm, Sweden

www.facebook.com/johnblakebooks 
twitter.com/jblakebooks 

First published in paperback in 2023

ISBN: 978 1 78946 410 8

British Library Cataloguing-in-Publication Data:

A catalogue record for this book is available from the British Library.

Design by www.envydesign.co.uk

Printed and bound in Great Britain by Clays Ltd, Elcograf S.p.A.

1 3 5 7 9 10 8 6 4 2

Every reasonable effort has been made to trace copyright-holders of material reproduced in this book, but if any have been inadvertently overlooked the publishers would be glad to hear from them.

John Blake Publishing is an imprint of Bonnier Books UK
www.bonnierbooks.co.uk

*We dedicate this book not only to all our extraordinary contributors but to all the brave women and men in the armed police and close protection world. Everyone that we met demonstrated courage, humour, grit and a sense of duty that will stay with us always.*

# CONTENTS

## Prologue:

# OPERATION STORT

One false move and the fifth in line to the British throne would end up dead. The only thing standing between safety and disaster for who had become the world's most famous royal after his grandmother were his close protection officers. Vigilant, discreet, highly skilled and fiercely loyal, they would not hesitate to put their own life before Prince Harry's. They just had to make sure it never came to that.

### 7.30 a.m. Friday, 6 March 2020
### Northampton armed police HQ

Superintendent Sarah Johnson stands calmly at a lectern in front of a packed room. The hubbub and chat dies down as she starts to address the audience. Strip lights above, rows and rows of plastic chairs. It could almost be a school assembly until you look at the people and remember the route into this place. High metal gates, CCTV, a guarded military compound. We are in the main briefing room of an anonymously situated, terrorism-proof armed police range complex.

Behind Sarah as she stands facing her officers is a screen with a photograph of Prince Harry, the 'principal' at the heart of this close protection operation.

Paperwork is distributed to each officer. Every piece is marked 'secret, do not share'. At the front of the room are four police bike outriders in yellow jackets who will escort Prince Harry in his armour-plated Range Rover from the county border to Silverstone. Great slabs of men. They have rugged, often worn faces and concentrate intently as Sarah is speaking. A further four plain-clothed close protection officers are in the front two rows, tough, muscular-looking guys with military bearing.

Even plain clothes is a uniform of sorts. Each officer sports stubble or a beard, blue trousers, pale shirts, quilted jackets and brown shoes with discreet sidearms in holsters, ear pieces and a calm composure. Behind them are the uniformed armed officers. Dressed all in black and equipped with body armour, guns and a Taser. These uniformed officers would be the ones to react with force should there be an incident. It is the role of the close protection officers to whisk the principal away, leaving the uniformed armed officers to deal with the threat. Finally, and behind them at the back of the room, are the unarmed officers, there to keep an eye on any crowds and carry out basic policing.

It might be first thing in the morning but there is a palpable sense of excitement and tension in the air. It is one of the final royal duties being carried out by the prince before he steps down from his position, and the buck stops with Sarah Johnson. She needs it to go without a hitch, and she calmly, efficiently works through her briefing explaining the many aspects and facets of choreographing and organising the close protection operation of a senior member of the British royal family.

The Duke of Sussex will be escorted by a fleet of motor-cyclists from Junction 9 of the A43, the border of North-amptonshire, to a venue inside Silverstone. Harry will be driven in a 2019 armour-plated Range Rover with a second Range Rover Discovery behind him as a back-up vehicle. When he gets to the venue, he will meet Formula One legend Lewis Hamilton. As Sarah explains, this comes with issues. Lewis Hamilton is not a protected person. However, he comes with a bigger entourage than Prince Harry.

When Harry arrives he will get out of the Range Rover and get into Lewis's car, who will then drive him to the front of the main Silverstone venue. Lewis has previous for driving a little bit too fast and for taking passengers in his car on impromptu drives at high speed around the track. The venue's management and the police have taken steps to prevent this from being possible today by making sure the track is in use and ensuring that there is very little fuel in the car Lewis will be driving.

Harry and Lewis will drive to the front of the building where they will be met by a group of school children and media. There will be blockers at each end of the road and no public will be allowed to get close. Silverstone have paid to install extremely expensive counter-terrorism bollards that slide up and down and would protect the principal from any kind of vehicle-borne threat, but at the moment they don't want to put them up.

The close protection officers will be plotted around the building. It is a single venue visit. All the people inside the building are named, tagged and vetted. There has been a search advisory counter-terrorism report carried out on the building. Sarah and her teams have spent three weeks planning this visit. They have been watching the media to see how much attention it has been generating.

Before Sarah starts there is talk in the room about *The Crown* and the parallels between Meghan and Wallis Simpson. Everyone has been following the news coverage of Harry and Meghan and there is a palpable sense of excitement. Even grizzled armed police officers are not immune to the power of these weapon-grade global celebrities.

Sarah begins.

'Good morning, everybody. For those of you who don't know me I am Superintendent Sarah Johnson. I am the tactical firearms commander for today.

'This is Operation Stort. It relates to the visit of HRH Duke of Sussex. These are some of the last of his public visits and therefore have drawn more publicity than ever.

'Another person of interest who will be attending the event is Lewis Hamilton to represent F1.

'In terms of threat we have some threat associated with right-wing terrorism and left-wing terrorism. There is no credible intelligence to suggest that an attack is planned or likely at this event. However, our overall national threat level is still Severe and that means that an attack is considered highly likely.

'I will cover the fixated [obsessed] persons at the end of the briefing.'

Sarah then goes through the technical police jargon associated with an operation like this. Police powers, the Human Rights Act, the Firearms Act, the Public Order Act. The circumstances when a firearms discharge is allowable. Then she outlines the command structure for the day with Sarah in the control room. The operational firearms commander (OFC) on the ground gets introduced followed by the other key officers.

There are five phases to this operation:

1. The collection of the principal and escorting him to the exchange point
2. High-profile drive-in with Lewis Hamilton at the venue

3. Being shown around the venue
4. Taking the principal back to his vehicle
5. Escorting the principal and entourage back to the county border after which the Met Police are responsible.

Each phase is planned down to the minute. Photographs have been taken of every section of the day to familiarise the officers in the room with the plan. The building is described in armed police language. 'Whiteface' means front, 'Blackface' is the rear. Maps are pored over and every movement discussed and double-checked for clarity. It is extraordinary to witness and a real insight into just how professional and well organised the British armed police are when they run a close protection operation like this.

The final part of the briefing is almost the most fascinating as it is given over to 'fixated persons'. These are individuals who are obsessed with the principal and part of the duty for the officers today is to look out for these people. There is a woman from Wembley who continually writes letters, an Indian man who keeps being arrested for pretending to be the Prince's royal protection officer in Windsor; there is another woman who is utterly sexually obsessed with Harry. Their photos and descriptions are shown on the big screen and all the officers pay close attention.

That is it. Sarah thanks everyone and walks to Silver command to run the operation and each of the plain-clothes armed officers, uniformed armed and uniformed unarmed go and play their part in this meticulously planned day.

It goes without a hitch. The next day Jonathan asked Sarah whether anything amusing happened. She smiled and said that a crowd of the public did form.

'Sadly for Prince Harry, they mostly seemed to have turned up to see Lewis Hamilton!'

# CAST MEMBERS

**Codenamed Walrus** – an elite bodyguard who runs a private army for an international billionaire who is a household name. The best of the best, Walrus spent sixteen years in the SAS running operations all over the world. We promised to keep his identity a closely guarded secret in return for him contributing to this book and we are grateful for his service.

**Codenamed Josh** – a former Israeli soldier who has spent decades looking after politicians, VIPs and even Chief Rabbis.

**Piotr** – the Polish man mountain, a 'unit' whose physical presence alone usually daunts trouble-makers into submission.

**Valery** – a Latvian bodyguard and former policeman who has looked after everyone from potentates to Hollywood stars.

**Rik** – the charming surveillance expert. From revealing serial infidelity to busting corrupt gangs ripping off big corporations, he has seen it all and expresses it with infectious humour.

**Ivan** – a bodyguard himself, this steely seventy-something runs his own close protection agency and knows this hidden network like nobody else. His elite core team is in charge of protecting HS2.

**Laurie** – a second-generation close protection officer, he has looked after prime ministers and major politicians, just like his father. Now he's the final hurdle on a gruelling twelve-week close protection training course.

**Ejeneca** – a bodyguard and driver whose first job was close protection for a member of the Bahrain royal family. Ejeneca is straight talking with a heart of gold and has proven she can hold her own in a number of different hazardous scenarios.

**'Lucky' Andy** – an ex-police officer turned surveillance guru. One of the very best at what he does, Andy sails close to the wind, including an arrest for kidnapping in the course of protecting a top former boxer.

**Codenamed Brett** – a tough former cop responsible for looking after some of America's brightest stars.

**John** – the epicentre of the British close protection world and director and founder of its toughest training provider, Excellentia.

**Sarah and Chris** – a husband and wife team with a

twist: both are top police officers and both are trained close protection officers. Sarah ran the Prince Harry operation, amongst many other big jobs; Chris did close protection for royals at the Olympics. Sarah challenges many traditional stereotypes of armed policing, and commands fierce loyalty from her teams of armed officers.

# INTRODUCTION

A significant, quietly compelling figure in the 2014 ITV documentary series set inside Broadmoor Hospital was the head of security, John Hourihan. Jonathan was the Creator and Executive Producer of the ITV Broadmoor series. John was charming, well spoken, slim, fit and immaculately turned out in Savile Row suits, with a firm grip and a laser-like stare. John was not exactly the shaven-headed screw that we expected to be running the gates and locks. Photos of senior members of the royal family around his office intrigued us further. John's last job before Broadmoor was as chief bodyguard to William and Kate. As Chief Inspector John Hourihan he had worked with the couple for five years, protecting them from Borneo to Africa. Prior to working with the royal couple, John had been personal protection officer to the Earl and Countess of Wessex. He had experienced many recces and foreign trips in the line of duty as Chief Bodyguard.

According to *Hello!* magazine: 'John, who managed two teams of four bodyguards, is known for his charm and discretion. The bodyguards are experts in marksmanship, close protection duties, first aid and essential diplomatic skills.'

We were drawn into the secretive world he inhabited before coming to Broadmoor, the planning, the meticulous attention to detail, the discretion, as well as the courage and bravery required to deal with a dynamic and ever-changing situation on the ground. We kept talking about him and his former world. It felt like another compelling one to explore, so over the last three years we set out to identify and talk to the most interesting and hard-to-reach members of this highly private community.

Imagine knowing that when you get up in the morning that could be the day you have to take a bullet or shoot a deadly assailant. How does that even feel?

In 2018, Jonathan executive produced a two-part series for ITV about the armed police with documentary presenter Ross Kemp. Before Ross and the rest of the production team came on board for all the filming, it was Jonathan's job to line up and secure all the extensive nationwide access needed to make the series stand out.

He started the research meetings with police up in South

Yorkshire, then he spent some time with cops from the West Midlands; he went to the City of London, then to the British Transport Police armed unit, up to Newcastle and even down to Devon and Cornwall. He met and talked in depth with all these different armed police units.

Sometimes it was just a meeting. Other times, though, he went out on a shift with armed cops. The first episode with Ross was all about what armed officers actually do and the threats that they face. Then in episode two we asked the question should all police really be armed and whether the era of the unarmed British bobby had come to an end. The hard-hitting two-parter covered everything from going out with a newly qualified firearms officer embarking on her first shift carrying a gun, through to MAST (mobile armed support to surveillance team) operations with the elite counter-terrorist specialist firearms officers. As close protection is a branch of armed police, this show became one of our entry points into this world.

It turns out that all police bodyguards are armed officers first. This was news to us. First you have to earn your stripes as an armed officer and only then are you able to try and be selected for the bodyguard training programme.

We were fortunate on the TV series to have two great ex-police officers as consultants who knew everyone and, significantly, had a strong relationship with the national lead for armed policing, Simon Chesterman. He sits on the COBRA emergency committee and is a well-liked and highly respected senior officer. Having the blessing of 'Mr Chesterman', as he was respectfully referred to all over the country, meant a lot. The jigsaw of this complex subject was beginning to reveal itself.

We had done two books previously, both giving access to compelling and private worlds, the first to tell the inside story of the Hatton Garden heist and the second the world of high-security hospitals in our book *Inside Broadmoor*, following Jonathan's 2014 landmark TV series about the psychiatric hospital. We love exploring these private worlds and finding out what it is really like to live and work in them. This felt like an exciting new one to enter.

In the second episode of the armed-police TV series we accompanied the police officers of Northampton, notably with some unarmed officers who had come up against knives and samurai swords in the line of duty. One of the officers we spoke to nearly lost his life after being stabbed in the leg by a samurai sword. That case was the one we were looking at as a tipping point for the series, to ask whether it is finally time to arm our famously unarmed police force. It was in Northamptonshire that we met Sarah Johnson who at that time was running the armed police division.

We really sat up and listened when series one of the smash hit TV show *Bodyguard* hit UK screens. It centred on the story of damaged war veteran David Budd who finds work as a police sergeant in the Royalty and Specialist Protection (RaSP) branch. He is assigned to protect the home secretary, the Rt Hon. Julia Montague MP. The first series was a huge success and it was obvious that the public shared the same fascination as us with what it takes to protect the rich and the powerful in our society.

The show offered a glimpse inside a dangerous and sexy world, but it is more than that. As we discovered talking to the real bodyguards, British close protection is regarded as the best in the world, the gold standard.

We were determined to find out more about this world and to meet the brave men and women who carry out this duty, for it is a duty and a calling. When it is done exceptionally well the work is completely invisible and it looks like they have done nothing; it is a thankless task.

We started with police bodyguards in our research then branched out into the private sector and this book delves into both sides of the industry.

In the 1980s, armed officers who were part of the Met's legendary unit, The Flying Squad, received one day's training before being armed. Now the basic course is twelve gruelling weeks. There is a 50 per cent failure rate. Trainees spend three days learning how to fire a weapon…and the rest of the course learning when not to pull the trigger.

How does it feel to do armed close protection for Hollywood celebrities? What was it like to protect Margaret Thatcher at a major international summit? We asked our contributors to reveal everything they could about what it feels like to be right inside events like this.

Fiction follows fact in the many movie and TV set-piece scenes in which a bodyguard makes a dramatic rescue at a political rally, rock concert or sporting event. We spoke to close protection officers who had been involved in everything from the London 2012 Olympics to the G8 summit to find out how it really feels to hold so many lives in your hand at these unique and historic occasions.

It isn't always a good story either. The very person we are all meant to run to when we are in danger has sometimes turned out to be a dangerous killer. There are also cases where police officers have fired, it has been deemed an illegal shooting and ended up in court with the officer being charged with murder. So we are under no illusions that this story has only one angle or that it is only a good story about bravery and valour.

As *Bodyguard* demonstrated dramatically, in this world there are untold dangers, close calls and blurred lines.

## Chapter 1

# THE HISTORY OF BODYGUARDING

The arming of police in Great Britain is a perennial topic of debate.

With the constant threats now posed by gangs, drug turf wars and terrorism, the world of the British armed police has changed almost beyond recognition for long-serving officers who remember how things were thirty years ago. The bodyguards' world has changed enormously, too.

As the Police Firearms Officers Association states: '*Throughout most of our history, the police use of firearms has been a taboo subject. The image of the unarmed bobby had to be preserved at all costs and some forces did not even admit that they had armed officers.*'

In Northern Ireland, all police officers are armed, unlike the rest of the United Kingdom, where only some police officers carry firearms: the specially trained firearms officers. This dates all the way back to the formation of the Metropolitan Police Service in the mid-1800s, when police were not armed, partly to counter public fears and objections over armed enforcers – residual brand damage caused by the British Army's often aggressive and coercive behaviour.

The aspiration for policing in the UK has been to have it be by respect and willing consent rather than armed force. World War I saw the increased arming of nearly every police branch across the UK, to mitigate against the threat of enemy invasion and sabotage by foreign spies. However, in World War II, police were only armed to protect the royal family and Downing Street. There were back-up firearms issued in case of invasion but the police did not take them on duty. After the end of the war virtually all the rifles, as well as significant numbers of pistols and revolvers, were withdrawn from the police service.

This set-up has been tested over time, with particularly awful incidents leading to calls for either more or fewer police to be armed in the UK. There was increased public appetite for all police to be armed in 1952 after a constable was shot dead and another officer badly wounded in the Derek Bentley incident (Bentley was hanged for the murder of a police officer despite not pulling the trigger), and also after the 1966 Massacre of Braybrook Street, which resulted in the deaths of three police officers in London and led to 17 per cent of London officers being authorised to carry firearms. The tide again turned though, during the 1980s, when there were a number of civilian deaths due to being fired on by police. These notorious deaths and the resulting public outrage contributed to the number of armed officers shrinking considerably. Those that there were had far better training and only received weapons under strict guidelines.

More recently, with the increase in terrorist acts throughout the world and in the UK, the question of arming the police has been brought more into focus. In 2019, despite the fact that more than 90 per cent of British police remain unarmed, there are now more armed policemen in the UK than there have ever been. However, it is unlikely that the British police will ever be fully armed. The police in England and Wales only fired seven bullets in the twelve months up to March 2016 and in a survey of officers in 2017, the Police Federation of England and Wales found that only 33 per cent were in favour of routinely arming officers.

Being 'armed', however, can mean different things at different points in history. Officers now have access to a range of items for personal defence, including CS or PAVA spray, extendable batons, and modern handcuffs called speedcuffs. Authorised firearms officers have also had Tasers issued to them for use against armed assailants since 2004. Then in 2008 the Home Office approved a roll-out of Tasers for all officers throughout England and Wales, simply stating that officers who have been trained to use Tasers form part of 'specially trained units'.

Ireland's history is different. When the Royal Irish Constabulary (RIC) was created in the early nineteenth century, following Ireland's absorption into the UK, it was a time of huge civil unrest between nationalist and republican groups. This meant that the RIC was armed from the get-go. In Northern Ireland, the threat from the IRA meant that male officers in the Royal Ulster Constabulary (RUC) were always armed, with females following suit only as recently as 1993.

Firearms were often deployed during the Troubles, which lead to the deaths of many people by firearms or plastic bullets. Twenty years ago, the RUC became the Police Service of Northern Ireland (PSNI) and remained armed. The PSNI have more wide-ranging anti-terrorism powers through various acts of parliament to the rest of the UK, and the officers have access to a wide range of weapons, not just firearms and Tasers but water cannons, CS spray and attenuating energy projectiles.

When Police Scotland was created in 2013, the first chief constable approved armed response vehicle (ARV) officers overtly wearing handguns rather than concealing them. The British Colonies, however, had similar police forces to that of Ireland. The Canadian Mounties, Shanghai Municipal Police, the Indian Imperial Police, British South African Police and other police forces of the colonies were all armed at various points and to various extents.

There are some places where you are more likely to encounter armed police as routine. The British Transport

Police were granted a firearms licensing exemption in 2014. You have standing authority to carry a personal firearm if you're in certain areas in an ARV, if you're on protection duties, or at high-risk sites like airports and nuclear facilities. Almost a decade after the exemption came into force, it remains a minority of highly trained British Transport Police, the Authorised Firearms officers, who are armed, and deployed only at key places in the network or in situations of heightened threat level.

British law allows the use of 'reasonable force' to stop a crime or make an arrest, but firearms officers can only use their weapons to prevent an imminent threat to life. Whatever the prompt for that, the police officer knows that they will be expected to be able to defend their actions in court.

Bodyguarding is an ancient profession, far older than the police service as we know it. Acting and former soldiers have always been the preferred hunting ground for close protection, even from the days of the Praetorian Guard who were responsible for protecting senior figures in the Roman army or administration. Introduced in a big and formal way by the first Roman Emperor, Augustus, around the time of Christ's birth, the pay was good and the headcount of bodyguards ran into the thousands.

Bodyguards had a less fortunate experience protecting King Harold at the Battle of Hastings in 1066. His personal bodyguards stood by him until the end when many other soldiers deserted, but it was not enough to save the king's life or prevent a French victory.

The Yeoman of the Guard were unmissable at the funeral of Queen Elizabeth II. They were an instantly recognisable, and very moving, component of the ceremony, demonstrating the latest act of loyalty in centuries of long service to the monarch. The Yeomen of the Guard were created by Henry VII at the Battle of Bosworth and during Elizabeth II's long reign they were known as the 'Queen's bodyguards'.

The royals, as we shall see later in the book, have had plenty of other close protection support as well. Queen Victoria had a favourite bodyguard, from the Irish Special Branch, for many years. Thanks to her excellent team, she survived seven confirmed assassination attempts and potentially dozens more that are harder to verify.

A recurrent theme amongst our contributors to this book is how important it is to have the trust and 'buy-in' of your principal, the person you're protecting. They have to allow you to protect them. Unfortunately this wasn't always the case. Abraham Lincoln had dismissed his bodyguard team the night that he was shot dead by John Wilkes Booth at Ford's Theatre in 1865. Indira Gandhi typically used Indian intelligence service officers for protection when she was Prime Minister of India. Unfortunately she went rogue and appointed some police officers from a different, unproven source. Two of them went on to assassinate her in 1984.

Another example is Lord Mountbatten. Prior to his death, when the IRA blew up his boat in 1979, he was warned not to visit Ireland. The shadow secretary of state for Northern Ireland, Airey Neave, had been assassinated earlier that year, and Mountbatten's close protection team warned him he was the likely target of a plot to assassinate a member of the royal family. His decision to disregard the advice cost him his life. Tragically other occupants of the boat also died: Baroness Brabourne and Mountbatten's fourteen-year-old grandson Nicholas Knatchbull, and Paul Maxwell, a local fifteen-year-old boy and crew member. This terrible event featured in *The Crown*, and these and other historic bodyguard and policing events have formed fertile fodder for TV and film.

## Chapter 2

# BODYGUARDS ON SCREEN

There is something inherently dramatic in the question of whether you would sacrifice your life to save another.

The hit 2018 TV series *Bodyguard* focused on damaged war veteran David Budd, who finds work as a police sergeant in the Royalty and Specialist Protection command, assigned to protect the home secretary, the Rt Hon. Julia Montague MP. In many ways he seemed like a barely fictionalised John Hourihan. The first series was a massive hit and it became clear that the public shared a real fascination with what it takes to protect the rich and the powerful in our society.

Richard Madden was an actor best known for his work in *Game of Thrones* before taking on the role of bodyguard David Budd. Budd followed a trajectory we have also seen in many of our contributors: a war veteran who becomes an armed police officer. Keeley Hawes co-starred as highly ambitious Julia Montague. The complex nature of the relationship between public figures and their close protection officers is at the heart of the story. With Montague's political views representing everything Budd is allergic to, he has to choose between her safety and his value set.

From the thrilling first episode it was evident that this was something very special. A nail-biting scenario introduces us to David Budd on a packed train into Euston with his two young children, Ella and Charlie, slumbering innocently in their seats.

Something we know from our contributors is that the state of hyper-vigilance that David is in is real. He notices everything, including plenty of things that others do not. A shady character tampering with a bin. A member of the railway staff checking on someone who had spent a bit too long in the loo.

After what appears to be the mis-identification of an innocent man emerging from the toilet, Jed Mercurio's fantastic writing twists in an unexpected direction. A terrified young female suicide bomber, Nadia, remains in the toilet and is discovered by Budd, apparently having been coerced into her lethal and murderous situation by her husband.

In the first of many complex and difficult situations that Budd faces in the series, many of which are familiar scenarios from the bodyguards that we met, he must decide whether talking Nadia down and saving her from being taken out by armed police is worth risking not only his own life but those of his children and everyone on the train. Can he get everyone evacuated on time, and will he escape with his own life?

The extraordinary and cunning act of physical courage that saves the day is the perfect introduction to the type of man that Budd is.

He is not without his flaws though. Damaged and haunted by his past, his drinking and erratic behaviour have driven his wife away. There is a nice moment early in his relationship with Montague, who also seems to drink heavily, when she offers him a glass of wine. He refuses: 'not on the job'. This type of self-discipline when it comes to their work rather than their personal life is something we saw time and again with the characters we met during our research for this book.

Much of the series' gripping tension can be credited to its composer, Ruth Barrett. Jonathan first worked with Ruth back in 2006 when they were both starting out in TV and they collaborated on Jonathan's first documentary as a director. Ruth composed all the music for it and they have been friends ever since. Jonathan has seen her rise and rise to become one of the top composers in the TV industry.

Speaking about the incredible first scene of *Bodyguard*, she explained that it was originally intended to be a much bigger stunt, set in Waterloo station. 'It ended up being quite a claustrophobic opening sequence because they lost their location. It made the show I think, it really drew people into that world in that moment of terror.'

Ruth experimented with sounds and synths in order to mirror the adrenaline and tension running through all of *Bodyguard*'s scenes. 'Rather than going really Hollywood with it, I chose to do something that was quite tense and subliminal and built in this really pulsing way', she explained.

Even when initially reading the scripts, Ruth could sense the high intensity of the show and the complexity of Madden's character. 'When it starts David Budd is just a normal guy taking his kids home and he has to suddenly be responsible for stopping this catastrophe from happening. And then he goes into the protection role and has to deal with the conflict of what he believes as a person and what Julia believes. But he has to be her bodyguard nonetheless.'

Ruth understands what makes Budd such an interesting character and what is a central point of drama in the show: he's in such a demanding, crucial job but is extremely troubled himself. Much of how she describes Budd's character reiterates what contributors have told us about their profession. Just like them, Budd is driven and able to react quickly to situations but, by contrast, he doesn't always maintain professionalism.

'He's such an amazing character to get into because he's quite dark and driven, he's good at his job but also bad and he crosses the line, and we like to watch those people.'

David Budd's traumatic past and his complicated relationship with Julia Montague add an exciting emotional tension to the show and heighten the drama of the incredibly challenging job that we have heard so much about during the research for this book.

The appetite for a second season was always going to be huge, bigger than anything else on television. In the late nineties there had been a handful of short-lived series that explored the profession, such as the immensely cheesy US series *V.I.P*, starring Pamela Anderson, or ITV's *Bodyguards*. These in no way garnered the same kind of attention as BBC's *Bodyguard* though. It seemed that Mercurio had mastered the appeal of the bodyguard on screen. Instead of the satiric portrayal of the profession in *V.I.P* or the melodramatic soap opera style of *Bodyguards*, Mercurio focused on the high intensity of the job and created a suspenseful edge-of-your-seat drama.

*Bodyguard* had been the most watched programme of 2018. Eleven million people watched the final episode go out, with another six million watching it on iPlayer. There could only be one PS David Budd though. Richard Madden had to come back. Nobody could write it except Jed Mercurio either. The pairing was TV dynamite.

Scheduling conflicts got in the way. Madden got snapped up by Hollywood. Mercurio was busy on his smash series *Line of Duty*. Finally, following the end of *Line of Duty* season six and with Madden having wrapped filming on the Marvel movie *Eternals*, they had more time. The series the world was waiting for might be able to get underway.

It's fun to ask our own cast members what they make of

some of these shows and movies. Sarah said: 'A couple made me shout at the TV – *Silent Witness*, *Line of Duty*. The first couple of episodes involved firearms teams. I couldn't watch it! I loved *Babylon* but that was a spoof. Same with *Hot Fuzz*, we liked that.'

For Chris: '*Bodyguard* was miles away from what the reality was, I couldn't bring myself to watch it. I'm struggling to think of anything I like.'

Our sharp-eyed contributors will pick up on errors that their training cannot let them miss. Latvian bodyguard Valery notices errors that real bodyguards would never make: mishandling their weapon, failing to properly check a crowd for threats, standing in the wrong place when the principal is entering a building or exiting a car: 'You see them holding a firearm up in a silly way: upright. It's ridiculous. These are people who look good as the furniture, not people who can save your life.'

The 1992 movie *The Bodyguard* was a romantic thriller starring the two hottest stars of the time, Kevin Costner and Whitney Houston. Costner played a secret service agent turned bodyguard hired to protect music superstar Rachel Marron (Houston). Critically mauled, its exciting subject matter nevertheless made it the tenth highest grossing film of all time at the time of its release.

*The Bodyguard* has even been adapted into a musical, which first made its debut in London's West End in 2012. Highlighting the popularity of the original movie, the musical has achieved global success and tickets are still in high demand. Whether this is a credit to Houston's music or the audience's interest in the profession is up for debate, but it's likely to be a combination of both.

In more recent years, the bodyguard as a profession has found itself once more on big screens; however, this time in a more comedic capacity. *The Hitman's Bodyguard* came out in 2017 and starred Ryan Reynolds and Samuel L. Jackson. It made over $170 million at the box office and throughout the film and in its advertising it poked fun at the seriousness of the character of the bodyguard in movies like *The Bodyguard*. It is an action comedy which follows the story of a world-class bodyguard hired to protect a hitman. It was followed by a sequel, *The Hitman's Wife's Bodyguard*. Thoroughly enjoyed by audiences, it demonstrated the appeal of the bodyguard across genres.

## Chapter 3

# WALRUS

**'A lot of times you're on your own and you know, there's no cavalry over the hill, the buck stops with you.'**

Sometimes a contributor comes along that stays with you for a long time afterwards. We wish we could say more than we can in this section but the job this man has is instrumental to ongoing national security. His need for absolute secrecy and anonymity is also a result of having signed a confidentiality agreement with one of the most famous billionaires in the world as his director of security. Codenamed Walrus, day to day he manages a private army of just under one hundred ex-special forces operatives to keep this billionaire and his family safe from harm in their many homes all over the world.

Walrus is very tall, slim but muscular, has long hair and is extremely handsome. We met at an exclusive private club in central London where, impeccably turned out in a bespoke suit and expensive shoes, he began by telling us about his early military career.

We wanted to know how Walrus got into the SAS, and, subsequently, close protection work.

He explained that to get into the SAS 'you have to be in either the British Army or the Commonwealth. You have to do a certain amount of years in any of the British Army or any other regiments, then you have to apply, but your regiment or unit have to recommend you. Walrus was in the British Army before the selection began. Following a recommendation from his unit commander he applied and went on selection.

'They have to say, "Yes, we think you're good enough to go." Then you apply and then you go on selection. It takes six months on selection, or just over. And it's every day. No days off. You start off on a hill phase, then you go into training for the jungle. Then you do the jungle. Then you do combat survival, and then you train enough to go to the squadrons. And then it takes three years to be trained up to be a fully operational guy.

'"The man" is the SAS,' he explains. 'It is a breed. It's the person and the personality as well. You come out as a product in the end.'

For the next sixteen years Walrus was full time in the SAS, carrying out top secret operations both at home and abroad from the first Gulf War onwards. He has been deployed in the Balkans, Sierra Leone, Colombia, Iraq and Afghanistan and he will take the details of these operations to his grave.

Walrus finally left the SAS after a period of three years of back-to-back operations. He was worn out. He was considering where he was going next and an opportunity came up to run a top-level private security firm looking after the safety and movement of the world's super elite.

Launching a top-notch private security firm was not a steep learning curve for Walrus. The skills that he has, working with different nationalities, different places, set him up perfectly for the work as an elite bodyguard. Movement and travel and threat assessment around the world all came very naturally to Walrus.

We had heard that these days the SAS are mostly deployed abroad.

'The SAS used to do big, really complex operations and high-profile stuff in the UK,' Walrus explained. 'But now especially counter-terrorism firearms officers do that in the SAS or abroad wherever. The SAS *is* still on the mainland doing things when it's appropriate or needed to.'

Some further training was required, though. The private bodyguard course and the police close protection (CP) training have some differences. There are the bodyguard courses and the SIA (Security Insurance Authority; the government body) licence. Once you have those two things, then you become eligible to work in the UK.

Walrus explained: 'This couple of courses, you can do abroad, you can use firearms. So you are trained on firearms and you go through all the aspects of the best course of one that's run by ex-SAS guys, right? Because you get more than just the basic training. You get a few more tips on what went wrong, how to do things to go about life, and just basics of how to get from A to B, how to travel.' For Walrus, training is both at home and abroad. He insists on both for new recruits to his firm.

Running a billionaire's private army, Walrus knows all too well that weapons are not allowed in the UK when you are looking after clients, but as soon as you step out of the UK it's a very different story, as he elaborated. 'SAS guys are used to getting around the world with nothing, just using their connections on the ground and moving with confidence. If any weapons are needed you can call on these connections. You need to know people everywhere.'

He described what he offers to his clients as seamless security combined with *movement*. From the cars to the helicopters, it is about travelling safely and smoothly without a hitch and without the clients even noticing.

He put it this way: 'You can't carry weapons in the UK, I don't know any people who actually do, even if they say they do. I'd definitely know if they were there, the police are coming and checking records so that they are sure, which is a good thing.

'You step out of the UK, it is a different story. This is the issue that when people employ security companies, you have got to look at the background of these guys. In the SAS guys are well travelled. They get used to getting around the world. Their contacts are the people they've gone back to. The people they've met on their travels. Different organisations, FBI, CIA… GROM, who are the Polish special forces.'

The acronym GROM that Walrus refers to translates into English as Operational Manoeuvre Response Group but also means 'thunder', and there is a great deal of respect worldwide for these Polish elite special forces. Walrus expanded on this: 'You would know somebody in the area so you can get some ground information. That way you can move around pretty easily, with confidence. And if there's anything needed, you can always call on those people with the right accreditation, with the right weapons. Because the last thing you want to do if you go abroad in these places, is turn up as a security company and you're carrying weapons, the local security company soon find out, and then the police will lift you because you weren't there. It's a very small industry at that top end.'

It takes courage and intelligence to inhabit this shadowy world, but this is the network you need to deploy to arm yourself place by place, to protect your principal.

Being in the SAS also primes you for going on an operation at the drop of a hat. Notices to move are second nature for men like Walrus. 'You have different times and different notices to move. Sometimes you will be on training.

So you wouldn't do anything. With no notice, you won't have any options. Then you gear up to thirty minutes, notice to move three hours, or twenty-four hours' notice to move. So it depends on what cycle are you on. You work where you work most of the time, but once in those operations, wherever you will, or however long you are, you have no notice then because you are just on all the time.

'If the client gets up at eight, you are up at seven. If they go to bed at 1 a.m. you are in bed at 2 a.m.' It means having a 'go bag' packed and ready and being willing to put everything in your own life on hold until the operation is complete.

Walrus is razor-sharp and laser-focused. We can see why his high-profile client feels safe with him and entrusts the safety of their family in this man's hands.

Walrus recruits the new leavers from the SAS into his world but, he explains, you can't have too many at once. They are too good. You have to mix them with different people, ex-Scotland Yard detectives, for instance. This recruitment is strictly word of mouth only.

Emma wanted to know how Walrus stays mentally sharp. He responded that he reads and keeps up to date with current affairs but, he says, it is really about who you are. Inquisitive, sharp, aware of your surroundings at all times. It's in your blood, and looking at and listening to Walrus he seems like a rare breed indeed.

He is also very aware that you have to stay in the background. 'If your name gets out there too much, if you become a celebrity, you can't do the job you do, because you become a celebrity as much as the guys you're trying to look after. It doesn't work.'

After meeting him we entertained ourselves with our own version of *Where's Wally?* Where's Walrus? Looking out for him, always discreetly in the background, in news footage of his billionaire client. He would do anything to avoid drawing attention to himself.

There's a lot of grandstanding in his business, though, as Walrus is aware when he vets people for his own organisation in London. 'Most people you meet in my sector, they've all been in the SAS!' he explained. 'They will say they have done something with special forces. The actual reality is there's very few. I've actually been in a restaurant or in bars when people are talking about what they've done in the SAS and it sounds fantastic, amazing. But it just didn't happen because they weren't there along with the helicopter pilots and the deep sea divers. You've got a lot of fictional characters in this game.'

With fantasists like that around, you have to rely on word of mouth to get to the right people. 'If the word of mouth is good, that's awesome. "Do you know him because he's worked with somebody around the circuit?" I can always pick up a phone and ask somebody, "Is this guy for real? Is he good?"'

We wanted to know too if anything ever rattled him. After all, he seemed impossibly calm and poised.

'Just completely cool. Nothing ever phases me. Really? No!' Walrus laughed. 'No, no, you do feel anxious, but I think it's all about gaining knowledge. A lot of times you're on your own and you know, there's no cavalry over the hill, the buck stops with you. So it's not that I've never been anxious. I just stopped that feeling. I try to stay calm and relaxed.'

There are steps you can take to ensure events run smoothly, he told us. 'If you panic, it's all over. You have got to be that step ahead. You need to turn up. What's the longest I've gone without sleep? Since leaving the SAS eighteen hours. If you go away you're working for two weeks for twenty-four hours a day. You don't turn your phone off. You don't take a day off for the grocery store.

'The mark of success is when nothing has happened, because you've foreseen everything, you've seen off everything, you've avoided something. If it's like that – seamless, silent, discreet organisation and planning – then it results in a good day. That's a great scenario.'

The worth of having someone like him can also be questioned. 'It is amazing when people you have worked for, for a while, start questioning – because nothing has happened while you're there! That's the balance you have to play all the time. There's nothing uncertain because we've *done our job*.'

You learn all kinds of tricks of the trade too, Walrus added, to make you a better bodyguard. He advised: 'When you go on a flight you never do hold luggage, always just hand luggage, roll your clothes, don't fold them. So they don't crease and you can fit much more in of them.'

When Walrus sees a VIP coming out of the car, he describes it as a scene that is set. It is about knowing what is going to happen before it happens. Where to look, where the risks are, how to head off an attack before it becomes critical. Even so, mistakes and tragedies can happen.

PTSD is an issue in the SAS. Only in the last week when we met Walrus a friend of his had died, and another committed suicide the year before. That's from a small unit and there's been a few more of those as well. It is not a new phenomenon. It's always been there.

'The way we dealt with it at the time? We saw some horrific stuff we were involved with. It's not nice stuff, what you're doing. We're there to do the job and it's the front line. Especially in the peacekeeper missions as well, you have displaced people, and women and children.'

When they got back, he said, 'They went on the piss for a couple of days and talked about it. Get it all out and talk it all through. What problems you had, how it went, get it all out of your system and then move on to the next mission, the next operation.'

If a man doesn't do this, Walrus explained, they can get lost. Though Walrus acknowledges that they are much improved from when he started out, the support mechanisms can only go so far. Addiction issues emerged in his unit…alcohol, drugs, sex. You are trained to have self-esteem, dignity, for that to be how your brain works. There are limits though.

A cerebral, brooding and introspective man, Walrus thought carefully when we asked him if there were any scenarios over his military and bodyguarding career that he would have played out differently. He paused for a while before responding.

'I think not actually on the ground when I was there doing them at that time, emotional, but going back in hindsight, there are different things.'

Walrus explained that looking at the bigger picture, there were some scenarios that he would have approached differently.

'It doesn't always go smoothly. It doesn't always go seamlessly. So there's regrets, no regrets in that way, but if you're looking back at history, the things that are dead, because you can't change history when you're on the front line…

'When you're in a different country, though, in different languages and different cultures, those things can escalate tenfold pretty quickly. There's always that synergy to look for where you and the police can get things done. And I don't mean it's not for the back door, but it's easy to pick up the phone saying, "This is wrong. Can you help us here?"'

To begin with in his private security work, Walrus had

several clients whereas now he just has one exclusive full-time client, running his private army. Clients at this level want the familiarity, the same person, the continuity, and hate change. Each client will have a specific guy allocated.

It's a small industry because there aren't that many people at that status and level that require the kind of inner and outer ring of steel and security that Walrus provides. As Walrus points out, though, there is more of this activity than you might think.

'Yeah. I think you'd be surprised. These days, there's quite a lot of this. It doesn't have to be at any particular level of wealth. It's just people's perceptions of where the world is now and what they want and how they want to live in it. What people are looking for is a seamless link between security and operations, from the money that pays for the helicopters to the way you go about your business. So people don't want the word "security" but at the same time they understand that they have to have it. It's about educating them in what it means, and it's not just one guy stood outside a car or following somebody.'

That is completely not what security is about, he went on. 'It's pre-thinking, a thinking man's game on your feet, knowledge studying, and also background information. A lot goes into it. There are those skills that you need to have as well. Medical skills, driving skills, but going back to that point, it is the man on the ground as well. So what about the money? If you get the right man, it's security, it doesn't have to be the biggest man. But he's got to be rounded in how he uses his brains. He has got to be smart.'

You can tell by Walrus's language that the world he inhabits is still very much a man's world. While we had met extraordinary women like Sarah and Ejeneca while writing this book, the tough existence of former SAS soldiers remains an ultra-macho one.

Walrus has had to balance the competing needs of his different clients. 'You can't be in the same place twice.'

Working exclusively for someone has made things much easier in that sense. 'When you get personal with somebody new and deal with them direct, you're the sole person and you can never change or just go back. You have a lot of familiarity with the same people and it's easy for them and for you in the end.

'This familiarity creates safety because to try and parachute into a situation – different places, different cars – you can mess up really bad. So we quickly learned that. Each client wants a specific person they'll stay with to service the project.'

When Walrus set up his company he had friends and colleagues from the regiment to do it with, but they often required surprisingly delicate handling.

'You have to be careful with the guys from the regiment, because they are high octane and highly paced, but they need a certain amount of freedom to operate as well. When you are in a company running stuff, there is only so much you can do individually. Unless you have got a hell of a lot of clients that need *that* at *that* time, you have to spread it out a bit with different people, like ex-Scotland Yard detectives who work in the company. Part of it is to get from A to B quicker than the normal person. In this country, for example, you can do that if you fly in a private jet.'

This demanding but glamorous world is not a million miles away from the sharp end of close protection, the real-life equivalent of David Budd's world, where terrorist threats must be identified and countered. The heightened awareness of threat is the same.

Walrus's vast experience has given him an interesting global perspective too. 'There are some great security guys out there but there are some really bad ones too. It is okay in their own country but very few security guys are good at travelling. The French guys are good in France, same with the Americans in the US. But knowing how to react and behave in a foreign country, outside of their comfort zone, is another thing.

'You might be in Argentina on a Monday, then fly to Paris, then to the beach in the south of France, then skiing in Switzerland. Next day, you're walking around, going to a concert. And the next day you'd be in a big crowd and, from all those facets, you've got to adapt to every single one, and every single one is different. You need a thinking mind to do that, and you need to be able to put your own life on hold. You have to adapt. Each scenario is different. Very few men can deal with that.

'So, you can parachute into different areas and put your lenses on the culture. When you go to Berlin, it's a completely different culture than London, and therefore a different way to operate. Then in Switzerland or France it's completely different again and you have to adapt. If you don't know how to adapt or you have not gotten a feel for that area, you will end up showing yourself up and you get it all wrong.'

Walrus explained that the ex-special forces guys from different countries might have very different styles but there is a lot of mutual respect at this level. Americans are very relaxed and accommodating in the US, relaxed and happy. However, in Egypt for instance, in his view the Americans are flummoxed, they don't know how to react and everything is very tense. 'If you're close and they just stand up most of the time, you can tell straight away. It should be about blending. Most of all it is always about being a part of the scene instead of being the scene.

'Israelis are the same. They have their own doctrine and style and they don't change it around the world. They do their own thing. The SAS looks at the situation and changes to the environment. This is why the SAS is the best regiment in the world, as they are generalists as well as specialists. It is about knowing which cars to use locally, how to speak the language, local customs and taboos. It comes from years of experience undercover.'

After all, Walrus was in the SAS for sixteen years.

He was, he told us, 'one of the youngest guys to pass

selection. At that time, I was nearly twenty-three and then in the winter I was straight to the first Gulf War. So, it was a post and then I was looking to hit every major conflict up into a post: the second Gulf War, Iraq, Afghanistan, the Balkans, Syria, Colombia.'

With this astonishingly demanding, sometimes brutal existence, there has to be a shelf life, as Walrus explained. 'Really you can do twenty-two years max in the SAS. Retirement age fifty-five at the latest. That said, in most units you can actually extend, it depends where you are, where you get to that rank or where you want to be. You can extend five, ten years and you could stay a bit longer in an operational role, more of a desk role.'

For Walrus, the SAS was addictive. 'When you have a collective bunch of people that have the same outlook as you, the same training as you, you get disappointed if you're not on form and on point, if you don't get picked for the operation, you want to be there. You just want to be a part of that group. But doing back-to-back operations for years and years... twelve months or six months and training operations.'

It is exhausting, physically and mentally. 'When your body gets worn out, your mind gets worn out. You get to a stage in your career. An opportunity came up to start a new challenge, and it was more than the standard close protection opportunities.' This was the moment when Walrus embarked on the successful career in private sector close protection that he had brought to life for us.

For Walrus, as for several of our contributors and sources, 2022 brought a fresh and unexpected challenge: the conflict in Ukraine. Russia's invasion had a profound and lasting impact on their client base. Oligarchs from Russia and other parts of the former USSR such as Kazakhstan and Uzbekistan, understand that close protection is a necessity, and one that they have pockets deep enough to afford. With many of these individuals going to ground, the future of close protection work for elite bodyguards in London and elsewhere has become more uncertain.

## Chapter 4

# JOSH

**'A good protection officer has to be like the modern man. Superman when he needs to be but sensitive other times. Invisible and discreet.'**

Josh (he requested a code name) is a former Israeli soldier who has spent decades looking after politicians, VIPs and even Chief Rabbis. He's an imposing physical presence. Strikingly tall, broad-shouldered and, like many of our contributors, charismatic, charming and magnetically attractive. There is a stillness about him, but it's the stillness of a loaded gun.

Much like another one of our codenamed contributors, Walrus, with his training in the SAS, Josh was built into the bodyguard he is in the Israeli Defense Forces (IDF).

The IDF is the military wing of the State of Israel security apparatus. Its stated purpose is 'to preserve the state of Israel, to protect its independence, and to foil attempts by its enemies to disrupt the normal life within it. The soldiers of the IDF are obligated to fight and devote every effort, even at the risk of their own lives, to protect the State of Israel, its citizens and residents.'

The IDF was founded in 1948, and its service branches encompass the Israeli Ground Forces, Israeli Air Force and Israeli Navy. Every Israeli citizen over the age of eighteen who is Jewish, Druze or Circassian is required to serve, with some notable exceptions. Men are expected to serve a minimum of thirty-two months, women twenty-four months minimum.

Given the existential threats that Israel faces, IDF military training is second to none. Josh was in IDF special forces infantry unit. He was still in the IDF Reserves elements even up to a few years ago. Something else the IDF teaches you, very useful for bodyguarding, is that you have to be 'on' all the time.

In February 2016, Staff Sergeant Tuvia Yanai Weissman, aged twenty-one, was off duty and browsing a West Bank supermarket with his wife and four-month-old daughter, when two terrorists began attacking customers. Since he was off duty, the Nahal Brigade soldier did not have his service weapon, but fought the attackers bare-handed, and was mortally wounded during this act of courage when his training, not to mention his protective instincts, kicked in. He saved his young family and other lives in the process, and was posthumously awarded one of the IDF's highest honours.

There is a very special course, even in the midst of all this elite training, and Josh has done it. It's the one that the El Al airline protection officers do. The one which qualifies you to go on the planes. Although the target of numerous attempted hijackings and terrorist attacks, thanks to these protection officers there has only ever been one hijacked El Al flight…and even that involved no fatalities. Of course, some of this is down to their pioneering use of technology like anti-missile shields, but it's down to the brave and highly trained operatives quietly sitting on every flight, too.

That course could be considered the high-water mark of military training in Israel, and, aside from his ongoing reserve work, that was when Josh took his cue to leave. He was well-equipped for the first role he took on subsequently, private security in Israel. This led to work with some high-net-worth individuals, particularly jewellers. That network, in turn, led Josh to London.

Once he returned to the UK capital, Josh worked in protection on a voluntary basis for the Jewish community, including three of those with their head perhaps most above the parapet in Britain: Chief Rabbis. The work was conducted through the auspices of the Community Security Trust (CST).

The CST is a charity, there to promote good relations between British Jews and the rest of British society, and to eliminate racism, in particular antisemitism, by promoting research, helping victims, improving representation and facilitating Jewish life.

Part of the latter involves protecting Jews from antisemitic terrorism. The CST consequently works very closely with the Met Police. In Josh's view: 'The Metropolitan Police give a high level of very good training. They respected that we were serious individuals, ex-military. CST are doing it for free. I trained with the famous Commander Alan Perrier, known as "Fizzy", many years ago. Training at the Met was really nice, and there was a bonding experience, too, having a coffee or a drink together.'

As Josh describes it, the CST now is quite well funded, but it was 'a broom cupboard out of Woburn House' when he started. The CST work with everyone to improve security, especially going into orthodox communities under threat like Golders Green and Stamford Hill. The CST probably saves half a million pounds a year doing the vital work that they do on a voluntary basis for the top six Jewish politicians and so forth. In its mission to eradicate racism, the CST is also working with the Muslim community to tackle Islamophobia and supporting other faiths in need.

Josh felt the need to counter the sense that there was a lack of transparency around the, necessarily discreet at times, way in which the CST has operated. 'The CST is not a secret organisation, it's an organisation that has secrets. You don't have to make the argument for its existence anymore, unfortunately.'

What Josh is referring to was the PR mission required early on to explain why it was necessary to have a charity devoted to tackling antisemitism as well as Islamophobia and other racially grounded hate crimes. With the rise in attacks, there is no doubt for the urgent need for such an entity now.

Even when he was focused on his CST work, though, Josh was never '*just*' a protection officer for the CST. 'Everyone should be broad and wide. You want to have a dynamic discussion. You must have an environment where people can talk and criticise, to improve the quality of the protection you are giving.'

That's how you avoid mistakes in these incredibly high-stakes situations. As always with Josh, there's a sense that he is also constantly involved in other things that he is not at liberty to divulge, but that feed continually into his training and his thinking.

In his liaisons with the CST and the Met, Josh describes: 'A *lot* of debriefings after a lot of incidents. Part of that involved me really *studying* international attacks, what went right, what went wrong. There is a completely scientific approach taken by, for example, Israel and the UK. Put simply, you use evidence to improve procedures. Techniques are always being honed, tested, modified.'

Unfortunately, Josh has been close to some very live examples to learn from even on British soil. On 26 July 1994 there was a car bomb attack against the Israeli Embassy in

London, which injured twenty civilians after a car containing twenty to thirty pounds of explosives detonated, with a blast audible over a mile away. A second bomb was exploded outside Balfour House, Finchley, a building occupied by the British Jewish charity, the United Jewish Israel Appeal, injuring six people.

Josh is proud that it was work done by the CST regarding the Balfour House atrocity and the bombing of the Israeli Embassy which got the terrorists convicted. In this sense, we see once again just how close bodyguarding work can get to espionage, intelligence work and the activity of the secret police.

After Josh left the CST about a decade ago, he carried on protecting other principals. 'A lot of the work can be quite boring, tedious, mundane, with occasional excitement.' Unlike the TV shows and movies, in real life excitement is definitely not what you want in close protection (CP).

As Josh knows from experience, 'You work with the principal. Now, some of them love it. Princess Diana. I heard that she did training with the SAS and absolutely loved it. During the first Gulf War, lots of MPs got extra protection, even backbenchers.'

Most of them were very enthusiastic and compliant, and could understand the value of heightened security.

As Josh continues: 'With modern day VIPs, if you are born into it, then you know. Princes and princesses know they need to learn about security protocols. Most people learn to accept it. It can be quite intimate with these VIPs, too. On a training course, for example, you have to push someone roughly into a car. Speaking as ex-military, it's about putting a civilian into a minute of combat'.

It's important to let the royals feel normal, to keep them safe going about normal duties rather than forbidding them from activities. Not to mention that, in Josh's experience, sometimes close protection can draw *more* attention for something like a principal going out for a run.

Madonna getting papped out jogging with her stagey, hulking bodyguards is one thing. A royal, rabbi, or any VIP that genuinely wants to go for an early-morning run under the radar might well be safer without an obtrusive bodyguard presence than with it, but it's the kind of gamble that close protection are never going to like.

The eagerness of many celebrities to flaunt their bodyguards at every opportunity isn't just about safety either, it's conspicuous consumption, as Josh indicates. 'Good quality protection is usually *expensive*. You can see it with Harry and Meghan. Prince Harry will have all different teams. An "asset" can be anything from an individual like Harry to an oil field, or the Falkland Islands.'

Harry comes under fire a great deal in the British press over this complex issue of protection. In 2023, the Duke of Sussex had has request for a judicial review rejected, seemingly over the Home Office's refusal to let him pay for police protection.

Having lost his taxpayer-funded police protection when he and Meghan, the Duchess of Sussex, stepped away from royal duties in 2020, Harry has been funding his own security in his new country of residence, the US, and has stated that he is happy to pay for police protection on UK visits too.

Given the eye-watering expense of paying for such security, which the Duke and Duchess stated in their interview with Oprah Winfrey they were funding from the revenue generated by their Netflix and Spotify deals, it is hard to escape the feeling that Harry believes the threat posed to him, Meghan and their children, Archie and Lilibet, is very real.

Harry's visit to London in 2021 for the unveiling of a statue to his late mother Princess Diana, was followed by what appears to be an unsettling security breach when his car was chased by photographers as he left a charity event. Given the circumstances of Diana's own tragic death, these situations must always be highly emotionally charged at best for the prince. His frustration at not being allowed to fund his own police protection on such UK visits could well have lead to a high-court battle. This would represent the first occasion in modern history when a member of the British royal family has brought a case against the government.

On the wider UK versus US culture of security point, according to Josh, when you compare them to other global police forces, 'British police are very approachable. It is better for your principal if you start very softly. I have never worked in America. But I will say that the British

Prime Minister has one protection vehicle. *Maybe* two. The President of the United States has twenty. All the American protection cars are like tanks. In America close protection are built like man mountains.'

We wanted to know about that critical moment of vulnerability, depicted in *Bodyguard* at many nail-biting moments, when the individual being protected is going in and out of places where an attack is possible.

For Josh, if you are talking about the entrance and exit of a secure facility for a principal, 'the best-case scenario is in a secure building all the time.' The least? 'Him riding a bicycle with no protection. Close protection *hate* walkabouts too.'

This is a point about training, and vigilance. Josh is engaging and articulate about the personal qualities that go into building the perfect bodyguard, and that you need to vary how you bring those qualities from place to place. He believes, for example, that eye contact is important in Britain. 'You learn techniques like "the fence" to keep people where you want them.'

'The fence' is putting up an aggressive barrier between you and an assailant out on the street. Pioneered by the brilliant writer, martial artist and defence expert Geoff Thompson, it's a method that controls the distance between you and your attacker, and consequently controls the situation, ideally defusing it decisively, before a dangerous altercation starts. Keeping the arms outstretched, directed at the upper torso, you maintain a distance of circa eighteen inches between you and your would-be assailant. The method also serves to block the path of punches and headbutts.

Seasoned close protection professionals like Josh know that the psychology of situations is just as important as the physicality, if not even more so.

'You have to have a character where you are sociable. You need to be a people person. You have to be really charming but also have an air of menace. You start at DEFCON 5 but you show that you can go up to DEFCON 1 at any minute.

Adaptability is key, too. 'You have to be seen as working with a family. You become very close to a principal, you learn their habits. It's very intimate. You're standing in the urinal next to them! I have had to wee into a bottle. Families I have protected are always very lovely, they wanted to feed me and look after me. It's about getting on with your principal but you also have to get on with other close protection officers. You always make sure you have the area sterile before the principal gets to the area.'

As we heard from the vast majority of our contacts in this secretive, heroic world of sacrifice, protection work is hard on personal relationships. 'It's very hard work with your own family though,' Josh explains. 'You have to drop everything to go to Israel or somewhere in a few days' time. I was in a very unhappy relationship. I slept on couches.'

It seems bitterly ironic that even as these brave individuals are pouring their minds and hearts, and even souls, into being the best protection they can be for individuals and their families under extreme threat, their own relationships and family lives are suffering and being drained of functionality. The corrosive effect of his work on David Budd's family life in *Bodyguard* is palpable in every episode, particularly the touching scene where he breaks down holding his children after a botched attempt to take his own life.

On a lighter note, Josh had all sorts of intriguing bodyguard life hacks that he was happy to share.

'Wet wipes are a trick of the trade. If you haven't showered for twenty-four, even forty-eight hours... Always have chocolate bars too, as you can easily go twelve to eighteen hours without food. You have to be resilient. Do a "tactical verification exercise": play fantasy mind games. This keeps your mind occupied when you are doing boring things.'

The element of sheer physical endurance involved in securing the safety of a principal 24/7 is pretty mind-blowing, and something only the best training can truly equip you for, as Josh indicated. 'You've just got to tough it out. Pop out press-ups to wake yourself up. Do some star jumps, that keeps you awake! The Queen's Guards *don't* stand still. That's a myth. They are actually rocking the whole time. Grab a snooze while you can. Being in a military unit teaches you all of those things. If you can nap, eat, shower or go to the loo *take the opportunity*. Experience teaches you that you can't be on red alert all the time. But you can be friendly, approachable, without giving information away.

'Going out on a shift I would look at myself in the mirror and say, "Today's the day Josh. It's going to happen today" to keep myself sharp.'

By 'it' Josh means what every close protection officer fears and prepares for mentally and physically every day. An orchestrated attack on their principal.

Close protection has been at the heart of many terrorist attacks of recent years. The British counter-terrorism police work in heavily armed SAS-style units, with highly trained marksmen deployed in key British locations to protect politicians, VIPs and innocent bystanders from the lurking danger of a sudden terror attack.

Police at the scene of a terror attack are usually the first responders, but authorised firearms officers (AFOs) in an ARV are usually the first armed police unit to arrive at the incident. In this sense, the British counter-terrorism police provide the UK's first line of defence.

As was seen in the 2017 Westminster Bridge terror attack by Khalid Masood, however, the first responder, before any ARV arrival, can be an off-duty close protection officer. Suddenly all their training has to kick in, along with the adrenalin, to let them neutralise the threat and save the day.

Josh has plenty of experience in counter-terrorism activity and knows all the signs to be alert for.

'Your best weapons are your brain and your eyes. Use them. What's the threat? The guy sitting at the bus stop when all the buses have gone past. Everything is a threat until you deem it not a threat. You have to be constantly like a tiger. You are getting to know your area, keeping it fresh. In a really life-threatening situation, you want to be ten to fifteen feet away with a pistol. Otherwise, what if he gets you?'

We wanted to know what action Josh would take in the event of a terrorist attack on, for example, a high threat VIP of the type he was protecting in the CST, or fictional Home Secretary Julia Montague.

'In the CST the first thing you say when under attack is "get down". Then you look up and if you can, *get away*. "Neutralised" means 5/6/7/8/9 rounds into the attacker's torso. You make sure he's not moving. If there is a clear attack, you have to stop that. *You can't allow the attack*. It has to be stopped. Quickly. Make the fuss on the street. It's about making your chances better.'

What Josh said next communicated volumes about the training that underpins the exceptional bravery of these 'bullet catchers'.

'As protection officers we are taught to run *towards* the shooter. If you can get someone, you get them.'

This is where the brain and the thinking enters into it, too. Every close protection officer and bodyguard we met was fiercely bright and hyper-vigilant. You have to be to outwit criminal minds and maniacs.

Josh puts it bluntly: 'Every attacker has a plan, so *you* must have a plan. Very few attackers have a B or a C plan.

It's not like the movies. It's about putting the reality of what you have to good use. If there is an attack happening, remember the MO of your terrorist, their information-getting routines. They will make sure that they know when the principal is coming out of the car. *It's a bit late when the bullets are flying.'*

Despite such displays of brain power and crime-solving behind the scenes, the key theme we could see emerging here was action. Your principal might be shocked or terrified into inaction during a terrorist attack, but that option isn't open to an elite close protection officer. You either run towards the shooter or run your principal away from them. You can't control your principal's reactions under threat...but you *must* control your own.

## Chapter 5

# PIOTR

**'Intelligence is more important here because in the UK you can't use a weapon.'**

Piotr is a Polish man mountain, 'a unit' whose physical presence alone usually daunts trouble-makers into submission. If that doesn't work, he has plenty more in his personal armoury. It's Ivan Stevens, whom we'll meet later, that described Piotr to us as 'a unit'.

'He's a big lad, six foot. Impressive size-wise and in the way he handles himself too. He's very calm though. He will de-escalate by saying, "You really don't want to put yourself in this position."'

Emma soon realised that she would have to take Ivan's word for it when it came to Piotr's appearance. Her meeting with Piotr was set up as a video interview. At the last minute though, after two anxious missed calls, and the fear she had been stood up, Piotr was on the line...but it was strictly camera off.

She was initially put out that the video call wasn't happening. Used to extreme secrecy, this nevertheless wasn't what she thought she had signed up to on this particular gig. Emma had spoken to plenty of close protection officers, responsible for some of the world's most powerful people. They had been happy to meet her in person. Or a VC at the very least.

What made Piotr any different?

But as Piotr's half-Polish, half-American warm, deep burr set in, though, Emma was captivated. Hypnotised. Soon enough, Piotr was making the kind of revelations where it was abundantly clear why he might be...camera shy.

He certainly started off extremely cagey, even in response to the mildest of questions, like where he did his training.

Piotr came straight back to reiterate that he was extremely limited in what he could disclose, including about his training in Poland – 'I can't say it all.'

'Tell me what you can say, Piotr.'

It was hard for him not to begin to warm up as he described the extraordinary experiences that had formed him into an elite bodyguard.

'I did quite advanced firearms. There are five steps, from basic to advanced weapons. It's a very different level of training. You're not just talking about target practice.

'Take "stress shooting" for example. That's where someone is throwing water, or sand, or stones at you while you
shoot. We had a Mossad trainer. We were three or four
Polish guys with an ex-Mossad officer. It was absolutely
amazing.'

Mossad is Israel's national intelligence agency, together
with Aman – Israeli military intelligence – and Shin Bet,
the latter essentially the Israeli secret police. Mossad's
responsibilities include counter-terrorism, covert operations
and intelligence collection. The director of Mossad has a
direct reporting line to the Israeli prime minister. Mossad's
training is world-renowned.

Piotr went on to describe how the training breaks down,
with five to seven trainees practising in two cities in Poland.
'There are two parts to the intelligence training and it is
really quite interesting. I love it, both parts, the surveillance
and the counter-intelligence. Our trainer had worked for
three different governments: Polish, Russian and American.
You learn how to follow, and how to disappear if someone is
following you. You also learn how to detect hidden cameras,
microphones and explosives.'

These are all critical skills in a close protection officer's
armoury. For the firearms training, there were more people
on the course, twenty, maybe even twenty-five trainees.
There were four to five trainings, for four to five days each.
That makes twenty to twenty-four days in total, a rigorous
process, but one that grants skills that could save a principal's

life. Then there was counter-surveillance which was taught in three different parts, for three days each.

Piotr explained that in terms of the qualifications, 'to get the badge, the licence, you need to do a course in the UK. Most CP [close protection] guys have been in the army or the police. So, it's interesting that I wasn't SAS, special forces or anything like that. I was proud of myself. At this point I was visiting Poland, but I was UK-based.

'Unlike the UK, in Poland you can use *loads* of weapons. Mainly Glock, sure, and the little one. The Kalashnikov.'

The Glock is an Austrian-produced semi-automatic pistol which has been widely used in military and police service since 1982, thanks to its performance and reliability. Kalashnikov is most renowned for its AK-47 gas-operated assault rifle, but it also produces a pistol. The latest version of the Lebedev PLK compact pistol has already been extensively trialled in the Russian Federation.

Piotr has learned to be very comfortable around firearms, but what about weapons for places where it's not possible to carry a firearm?

'I did loads of knife training. As defence you learn how to use a knife. There was one quite interesting guy who was working for the Russian government, he had his face covered the whole time…'

You can only imagine what sort of activities a top-secret Russian operative had been up to in order to become a covert knife-training expert in Poland.

Piotr made a really interesting point about what the biggest clients, under the highest threat level, actually want. 'With training, the big clients focus on first aid, not firearms. You have to know how to deal with stabbing, with shooting. I had no vehicle training either. We always had a driver. Under that level of threat you can't protect your principal from an attack or perform emergency first aid and drive at the same time.'

Piotr knows all too well that when working in the UK, without a weapon by your side, de-escalation is the name of the game.

Piotr was working at a large, glamorous casino in central London and soon came up against some situations where not being able to carry a weapon put him to the ultimate test.

Normally, casinos select and vet people on doors, but not this one. It is open for everyone. This was causing some hefty problems with the clientele. The place was brimming with drug dealers and prostitutes. The people who employed him there told Piotr it was going to be a three-month job to clear up the place.

Piotr had the place clean after three weeks. The general manager came over and complained: 'You've done a great job but business is going down. Can you be more flexible and bring a few back?!'

Piotr said this captures an interesting but tricky situation. In his view there is always trouble with the management; they don't care about health and safety, they just care about money.

The first time Piotr saw a big win he could see that there were a few plastic bags, gift bags – in total ten bags full of money. 'The guy who won the cash was alone, getting drunk and high. He started throwing the money all over like rain.' It was a pretty depressing sight, and a potentially volatile situation that he had to keep an eye on.

Another night the casino was buzzing, full of excitement about an imminent arrival.

'Benjamin is coming'.

Who was Benjamin? It wasn't easy to get the intelligence about him Piotr would have wanted from the other staff. He had a bad feeling about it.

When the mysterious Benjamin turned up he was hugging people on the door.

Piotr could see the shape of a gun on his back. Piotr decided to hug him too, to check him. Sure enough, he was wearing a weapon.

'Don't worry, everyone knows me.'

Piotr asked: 'Do you have any papers saying you are allowed?'

Benjamin replied: 'No, I'm not a policeman.'

Piotr said: 'No, we can't let him in.'

Under pressure from the staff, and with this obstructive response from Benjamin, in the end Piotr had to let him in, fully armed.

Another night, a group of Jamaicans came to the door seeking entry. Piotr indicated that 'the issue was the dress code. They looked like they came from the beach or the football pitch.'

'Don't you know who I am?'

Piotr politely asked the ringleader to leave. The ringleader responded by pulling a gun and pointing it at Piotr's head.

The manager came over.

Piotr recalled: 'He was holding the gun to my head for two minutes. That feels like a very, very long time when someone is holding a gun to your head.'

The manager eventually persuaded the gangster to stand down.

'They quit, and jumped into a big black van. The main guy pulled down the windows of the van, and said to me, "You're finished tomorrow."'

Piotr went home and drank an entire bottle of whisky while trying to decide what to do. 'My missus asked me what was wrong. When I told her, she said, "Don't go back."'

And there it is again. The pressure this job, the mission, puts on conventional relationships, both real and fictional: Valery's broken marriage (see next chapter). Josh's unhappy relationship. David Budd's marital breakdown, and the spiral it sends him on towards a devastating relationship with his principal, Julia.

What was the outcome though? Emma was desperate to know.

'Alpha male, right? I decided to go back.'

Piotr was back on the casino door again. Adrenalin pumping. The warning words of his worried wife echoing in his head.

The six guys came back. They came out of their huge car and they shook his hand.

They said: 'You came back – respect.'

As a bodyguard, you can't always rely on such a happy ending.

Piotr's longest job was for an Iranian family. It was an incredibly high-threat situation. How high-threat? Well, three or four crews had been hired for this one family. Piotr was inside the residence, then there was someone outside watching the residence. Then there was someone watching *them*. The residence was off Hyde Park, near Park Lane'. The family had two mansions, one there, one in Hampstead.

He clicked with the family straight away.

Piotr was originally sent during his CP course, to cover one night only. The family called his company and said they wanted him to stay longer. He was still in training, his employer responded! They told his company: 'We are the clients. Follow us or you lose the contract.'

After only three or four weeks he was team leader, in charge of SAS, Polish soldiers, special forces. The people Piotr was leading didn't like it because they were ex-military. The client didn't want a soldier in charge though, they wanted a civilian. He asked: 'Why me?'

The client's response was simple, and a reminder of what

Brent Library Service

## Customer ID: *******5386

### Items that you have borrowed

Title: Bodyguard : the real story : inside
the secretive world of armed police
protection
ID:    91120005076787
**Due: 06 February 2024**

Total items: 1
Account balance: £0.00
Borrowed: 5
Overdue: 0
Hold requests: 0
Ready for collection: 0
16/01/2024 18:07

it really means to these high-net-worth, high-threat families to let this level of security inside their homes.

'Soldiers don't have the heart, they don't have the common sense in a civilian environment.'

What does a statement like that mean in real human terms? The mother of the family was quite old. She'd arrived that first night, Piotr opened the door, and he took some bags for her. She really liked him straight away. The matriarch's opinion mattered. Sometimes in close protection, it's the little things.

Piotr was quick to point out that he's an educated man, too. He's a teacher. With three ladies on site and four kids, he organised different activities for them, sports activities. He was trying to give these children in this very high-threat situation a normal life. Other clients over the years have also really liked that about him, too.

Piotr explained more about the scenario.

'To show you how big a deal it was with these Iranians, Tony Blair was often on site. They were *very* rich and *very* important. With a family like that, you get lots of guys trying to charge £5k for twenty days to protect them. They're expensive but they fail at the work. For example, this residence. It has got loads of cameras. Say you see an older lady at the gate, if you send a soldier, he will escalate the problem. I did it differently. I asked questions nicely.'

They respected Piotr. But more importantly, they liked him and they trusted him.

Piotr had worked at the world-famous luxury Dorchester Hotel too. He was in charge of the guys securing high-profile events.

Inevitably, there were potential threats from people. Or were there? People begging. Drunkards. In close protection you have to be prepared for people not to be what they seem. Whatever was going on, the British guys couldn't deal with it softly.

One American colleague, who had been in Delta Force, explained why to Piotr: they are 'missing something'. 'If you go in for war, you are holding the weapon in your hands. You don't forget that in civilian life. They get nervous, and they end up escalating the problem.'

Formed in 1977, Delta Force is a special operations force of the United States Army. Elite and secretive, it's a tier-one counter-terrorism unit, designed to kill or capture high-value targets. Delta Force also protects senior US leaders on visits to areas of high threat, undertakes covert missions and hostage rescues.

Its most famous missions include Operations Red Dawn – locating and capturing Saddam Hussein; Operation Black Swan – the capture of Joaquín 'El Chápo' Guzman, the notorious cartel leader; and Operation Kayla Mueller, an audacious Syrian raid that killed terrorist Abu Bakr al-Baghdadi. Coming off missions like that into private close protection work, you tend not to have had that much time to work on your diplomacy and softer social skills.

It is clear that flexibility and agility are so important on these jobs, too. As we also learned from Ejeneca, Andy and Valery, as Piotr put it, 'clients have some *extremely* strange requests'.

Former SAS are *very* proud of being former SAS. Imagine a client asking them to walk the dog? They would refuse. Piotr, though, would say, 'Yes, let's go with the dog.' The Iranian family had thirty officers month by month coming and leaving. Most people only lasted a few weeks. Piotr survived for two years.

They wanted him to go with their kids to the swimming pool. You can't wear a bulletproof vest taking the kids to the pool or the park... For jobs as big as the ones he has worked on, you can't drive and secure people either. They had trained drivers.

'A high-threat situation like this is not a random with a knife. There are whole countries that want to kidnap the kids, it's all very organised. The Iranian family used to work for the Russian government. Gorbachev was at their wedding. The security team were getting paranoid, even about the sound of birds landing on the limo. Doing twenty nights in a row, your mind changes.' These highly trained operatives were in such a paranoid and fatigued state that they were jumping out of their skin every time a bird landed on the car, thinking it was a bullet or an explosive.

Due in part to his exceptional surveillance training, Piotr is an observer. He loves observing. For Piotr, knowledge comes from many different places. Someone he worked with called him 'a Hoover'.

'You can even learn from lots of stuff online, looking at notorious shootings, kidnappings and so on. That's how you learn. Body language, how you speak to the client is so important too. You have to be really careful with Middle East ladies: not just what you say but not even looking at them inappropriately.'

Returning to the Iranian residence, Piotr told an extraordinary story of being a bodyguard during a visit by 'a British politician. A politician on Tony Blair's level. British police were checking the residence with dogs, sweeping for explosives.'

He was covering the main door, so he had the list and was judging who could come in.

Someone had sneaked into the residence. Piotr opened the door with a small gap.

The person introduced himself as a police officer, and said he wanted to go in to use the toilet.

Piotr refused. 'This is a private residence, this is against protocol, you are not on the list.'

'I want to come in to use the toilet.'

'Sorry, you're not on the list.'

'I'm a British police officer, you have to let me in.'

Piotr continued to refuse.

Finally, the man put one hand on the door gap and jammed one leg in between. 'He was saying, "Where are you from? Are you crazy? Telling a British police officer what to do!'"

Piotr said he would close the door – that he had left him no choice. The intruder persisted.

Piotr shut the door hard with the man's hand in between, injuring him.

A personal assistant, responding to the loud commotion, ran down and shouted at Piotr. 'What the fuck is going on? You damaged the hand of a police officer?'

Piotr spent two hours waiting to know his fate, knowing he had failed, and that he was going to lose the job.

Eventually he was called to a conference room.

'It was amazing. There was a long table like in a Mafia movie and spotlights pointing on all the chairs.'

His client, the head of the family, came in, asked him quietly, very relaxed,

'Piotr what have you done?'

'I gave the guy three warnings, there is a protocol.'

The client responded: 'That was a police officer. What have you done?'

Piotr replied: 'You can buy a fake police badge'.

The client said: *That was why I picked you. Because you think differently.*

Piotr has worked for many other, very demanding, private clients in risky situations too.

'I protected two females from Qatar. They came to *party*. They were full of alcohol and drugs. Two attractive ladies. We were in a nightclub. There were these massive bodybuilders trying to hook up with the girls.'

That's the kind of scenario every bodyguard dreads. A drunken, drug-fuelled client, careless of their own safety, flaunting their wealth, inebriation and vulnerability and rapidly getting surrounded by opportunistic, shady and dangerous potential assailants. When clients are in that state, as we will learn from Valery and Ejeneca too, it's so much harder to get them out of a venue to a safe place quietly and safely.

These issues haven't just arisen for Piotr in London either. He's had difficult client gigs in Paris and had a nightmare in Monaco.

'I ended up in jail in Monte Carlo. I went with two clients to the beach, they were two beautiful Asian sisters.'

Piotr was keeping his distance, not wanting to draw attention to them on a public beach but ready to spring at the first sign of a threat. You can't let your guard down. 'If something's happening, you need good timing to approach. There were what seemed to be locals selling fake watches. They approached my clients, I was watching from twenty metres away. I was watching, I thought it was the right time, and suddenly one of the guys removed one of the ladies' bras.

'I ran the twenty metres and I threw my jacket over my clients. I shouted, "Go go go!" to the girls, who ran back to safety at the hotel.

'The situation blew up for me though. One of them crushed a bottle with his hand, it was a very aggressive fight. Nobody came to help either. I had to fight two guys. I didn't have a weapon.'

Piotr had to draw on all his training, quick wits and resilience during the attack.

'I used a chair and a bottle. Eventually the police came, and we all got arrested, I was in jail for eighteen hours. The watch vendors were Albanian criminals. Watches are just a hook-up though, it's not about that really. They want to see how rich you are, they are watching for you to make a mistake with lots of cash. Somebody paid for me to get out of jail. They opened the door at the police station, gave me the documents, and the rest of my stuff back and said, "You can go." I still don't know who bailed me out.'

For Piotr, though, the most challenging situation he has ever encountered is...babysitting!

Of course, this was no ordinary childcare gig. Two of the children from the extremely high-threat family wanted to go to a huge annual winter festival in London's Hyde Park.

'Honestly, that was my biggest ever scare. Not knives, it was being with the kids at Winter Wonderland. Can you imagine? Looking after the kids at Winter Wonderland, two kids running around with thousands of people. They wanted to go for one ride that lifts you up 100 metres high. The kids enjoyed themselves. For me it was like the electric chair. Also, the swinging boat. They wanted to sit at the highest end! I was so worried about being sick in front of them. You have to be flexible…but that really tested me to the limit.'

It's this absolute loyalty and commitment to a family's safety, in the face of a kind of adversity and threat most people are lucky enough never to encounter, that keeps someone like Piotr, or Walrus, or Josh, or Valery, or Brett, in big demand from many of the ultimate international close protection clients.

As a postscript, having gained his trust, Piotr sent Emma a couple of pictures and short films of himself. He was a bronzed, burly guy, with the physical presence that Ivan had described and a military bearing. He wanted to add something for Emma: 'I forgot to say! The main training for CP should be psychology.' Once again, no matter how big and strong they are, these bodyguards all conclude that their brain is the most powerful tool in their armoury.

## Chapter 6

# VALERY

**'I prefer one qualified bodyguard next to me than fifteen unqualified muscly guys.'**

Valery is a Latvian bodyguard and former policeman who has looked after everyone from presidents to Hollywood stars.

A stocky, highly physically intimidating presence, Valery carries himself like a wild animal about to strike, with a sense of controlled strength and lethal action poised when needed.

He is, though, also self-deprecating with a wonderfully dark sense of humour and perfect comic understatement. He has had a wealth of crazy international experiences and spent a lot of time working in the USA. The global comparisons he makes are unique, insightful, thought-provoking and often hilarious. His thousand-yard stare, though, communicates more than his words do about some of things that he has seen…and done.

As mentioned earlier, with both the fictional David Budd and virtually all of our contributors, devoting his life to close protection has come with considerable personal sacrifice. 'The work isn't good for family life. I wouldn't recommend it.'

After middle school, Valery had no idea that he would become a bodyguard. He was born in Latvia on the coast of the Baltic Sea. He attended police academy in Latvia, then entered the police force. After that, he moved on to special operations.

In contrast to Piotr, Valery trained in Germany rather than Poland. Also unlike Piotr, Valery's advanced training course included driving, as well as all the weapons training and tactical skills that you would expect.

The course in Germany was at the Münster police academy. In order to complete the course it is necessary to be either ex-military or ex-police. It is a two-week course constituted of 150 hours' work.

Valery described a range of very challenging scenarios that the trainees are put through.

'There were different exercises, like fountains spraying water so you lose control… They threw a mannequin at seventy miles per hour and you have to stop your vehicle one metre before you hit it. The driving has A/B/C categories of difficulty. You are training for fast reaction to a threat. From

206 trainees, only 92 passed, so there was a more than 50 per cent failure rate.'

Passing this course was a real achievement. Valery's wide experience has taught him that there is so much more to being an elite bodyguard too; you have to be a true polymath.

'Knowledge of the law is very important. I know people in prison for transporting things they shouldn't have done… They are British serving time in British prisons. Languages are important too. Chinese clients like it if you can speak Mandarin or Cantonese.

'There are other skills you can learn like skiing. In the mountains you have to ski with your clients. It's a good idea to get your PADI as a qualified rescue diver, so if your client likes scuba diving…'

Valery considered several countries but decided to relocate to the UK. He worked in a SWAT team at home, but then moved to Britain for better money. The bodyguard licence he had earned in Israel and Russia, following his training in Germany, is not valid in the UK, so he did a CP course in the UK and then worked as an instructor.

His training was first class, but in his view the CP market in London has since gone way downhill. 'I would skip 99 out of 100 CVs if I was hiring now: 60 to 70 per cent of companies offering bodyguards are fake. You only have to take a two-week course. That does not work. You must have police or military experience. You need a brain, an education. You have to be able to drive different vehicles.

You need computer skills. You need language skills. I have worked with CP officers who work with the BBC, with movie stars. You have to be highly skilled at lots of different things.'

As Valery explained, he can cover all sectors and do all aspects. He can teach everything from close protection transit operations to physical intervention. He did tutoring and then several short-term CP jobs. Between 2010 and 2012 he worked for the Chinese Embassy. They could 'afford any wages' for him and his team, who were working at the Portland Place embassy site. Then Valery worked for the Embassy of Qatar. The Qatari Ambassador had a big close protection team working with him.

We wanted to know why Valery thought he had been given jobs as big, responsible and lucrative as these.

'I don't drink at work, I don't touch drugs, I am never late. Most clients like *discipline*, so I started being recommended to people. My clients say I do it much better than other people. They are paying the money for actual *work*, not for the photograph of the big bodyguard next to them.'

His clients have certainly been diverse. In addition to the Chinese and Qatari embassies, he had a Hong Kong client and Russian clients in London – the latter a piece of business that may diminish given the conflict in Ukraine.

He spent time in New Haven, Connecticut too, and was struck by many transatlantic differences in close protection. 'In the States *everyone* has a gun. It is much riskier. It is surprising how many people are armed in the States.

You don't even need a licence in Vermont, you can just walk into a gun shop and get a firearm.'

Valery was once on the street in the United States and apparently looked like someone the police were looking for. 'They told me to put my hands down and I didn't want to. Every coroner could tell if they shot an unarmed man with his hands up. They shoot and then ask questions.'

You need to know how to carry yourself and defuse hazardous situations like that, and luckily Valery did.

Consequently, Valery explained, 'US versus UK, it's a different type of work. The potential risk in London is low. In the UK there is a style. The client wants to show they have the money. It's "a show off". It is not to do with actual danger or protection. In the UK close protection is status. It is psychological, it's all in their [UK protection] head. In the US, the secret service put on a big show of force. There is not the focus on discretion like there is in the UK.'

There is a difference in focus around weapons too. 'Even if you pass weapons training here...you get a firearms certificate. In some countries, for example Italy, Ireland, France, *only* police can have firearms. In Georgia, I went to the local police department and signed all the paperwork. This was 2008 and you got a firearm signed for you. You cannot use your own but you can get one straight away. You get asked millions of questions if you want a firearm in the UK. Barack Obama had fifty-seven, maybe fifty-eight bodyguards on one of his UK visits but only twelve had a firearm. In the UK they just will not let you have one, whoever you are.'

In fact, Valery would go even further. 'The situation completely changes as soon as you leave the UK. People are heavily armed in the US, Brazil, Argentina, Eastern Europe, Asia. Big muscles don't mean *anything*. If you are working for a principal in politics, even if you have clearance for a weapon in one country you still have to go through a vetting process elsewhere.'

Valery is well aware that you need to be a bit of a chameleon too.

'Information is worth more than gold and diamonds. When you are travelling abroad you have to learn the local ways. You need to get to know the landscape. The primary and secondary routes... Whether I am travelling to the US, Canada, Asia, I always provide a list of what I need. The client provides the bulletproof vest and other such necessary items.'

Planning ahead is important. 'Route planning, train tickets. This all takes days or more. The Middle East takes three weeks' preparation *minimum*. I know SAS guys. Those guys do their job perfectly. My work is all about avoiding a potential threat situation, *not* creating one.'

Much as this is Valery's aspiration, when you have hedonistic international private clients, wealthy beyond most people's imagination, who let their hair down when they're globe-trotting, then a potential threat situation can arise very rapidly.

One of his former clients was a Sikh multi-millionaire businessman.

'He had been hiring "greenhorns". These are people with no military experience but they hold the bodyguard licence. He was partying with another guy and his bodyguard and he got beaten up. The other bodyguard had started the fight!'

Greenhorns are usually a liability as far as real pros like Valery are concerned. Poorly trained individuals and an atmosphere where the client has come to party can present a major danger. It's a toxic mix. It is human nature that not all VIPs will accept that the protection they are offered is for their own good, especially when they are under the influence.

Valery has seen 'clients in nightclubs high on drugs, alcohol, spraying champagne. Dancing on tables and spraying it around. There were other people in the club who didn't like that. Some of these clients behave like little kids. Most of them don't recall anything in the morning. You cannot fight the whole club by yourself. You get paid for the safety of your client.'

On another occasion, Valery had travelled to Georgia as part of a team in which the client had three armed bodyguards. Even that level of protection is not necessarily sufficient though, when 'they drink five or six bottles of wine and do "silly stuff".'

Valery has seen this often enough now to know when to intercept it before it becomes dangerous or professionally embarrassing for his client. 'Half of the people, when you get them on the plane they are still completely drunk, they don't know what they're doing.'

The client in Tbilisi, Georgia was in bed with a woman and very late for a flight. He had been partying with girls all night and his flight was leaving in two hours. In the end Valery dragged him out in his underwear. He was drunk so Valery threw him over his shoulder in a fireman's lift and put him in the back of the car to the airport.

The client shouted, 'You're fired, bastard!' The client slept the whole flight to Moscow. After sleeping for four or five hours on the plane, the client kissed Valery profusely and thanked him. When he sobered up the next day he gave him extra money. He put Valery's pay up by £10k, and gave him £5k cash there and then.

With nowhere to meet in lockdown, Emma's first face-to-face meeting with Valery was in the ultra-glamorous location of the shopping aisles of a cavernous Tesco superstore in Potters Bar north of London. Huge and intimidating, Valery was keen not to wear a mask as he had received his immunisation jab while working in Russia. After a number of furious glances from elderly shoppers, he tucked away the Russian language immunisation certificate he was brandishing and wore a mask for appearance's sake anyway.

During the meeting Valery strongly echoed what others had told us. That the close protection world was not for family men. His marriage had broken down and he now visits his kids in the south of England when he's not working abroad, although Brexit and coronavirus had affected his mobility as it had everyone else.

From Valery's perspective, 99 per cent of people in the UK run serious legitimate businesses and they don't want trouble with the law. Globally is a different story though, and Valery has been close to a great deal of criminal activity during his long career.

Private clients ultimately want discreet protection which enables them to safely do whatever it is that they want to do. With wealth and status comes a sometimes unwelcome amount of visibility. You put your head above the parapet and you don't want it blown off. That is where close protection can come in.

Valery provided Emma with an interesting summary of ways you can earn revenue, if you are so inclined, as an international bodyguard. Some of them are things that he would never do, but he has seen many times.

## WAYS TO MAKE BIG MONEY IN CLOSE PROTECTION: ACCORDING TO VALERY

1. A private military company, be it American, Hungarian, British or some other country, is one way to make money. Plenty of his clients have a legal business but also something on the side: illegal oil, or a diamond business.

'A private military company is *always* through someone introducing you. You don't apply online! This is very, very highly paid, you are talking $150k to $250k per year. You can earn £1000s a day...but you might not come back.'

2. Then there is what Valery calls the 'ordinary normal businessman' client. 'They don't need a bodyguard, it's a lifestyle. You're part of the furniture, like an expensive car.'

3. Even further down the threat level there is what Valery calls a 'personal nanny'! 'There is absolutely no threat to this particular person. There are no parties, drugs, alcohol – just school, home, shopping. This person needs someone to help him do shopping, drive his car.'

4. One client asked him to carry a suitcase of drugs for him. The client offered £50k up front and £100k on arrival. Valery said no. This is another way plenty of dodgy bodyguards make extra cash, though.

Valery says in this shadowy world, there are many lies told on the news. There was one very high-profile guy, and Valery saw that the BBC reported he had committed suicide. Two days later Valery saw him with his son. He had gone into witness protection. He managed to get to Israel and then safely disappeared.

'If you have the money you can do whatever you want.'

A great deal of Valery's work involves surveillance and counter surveillance. For example, putting a tracker on a business partner who his client does not think is being honest with him. Surveillance equipment costs a lot of money and the client has to pay for all of this.

'A tracker has to be professionally done. That means done at 4 a.m. and you have to have your face covered. You must make sure that you cannot be identified.'

This is one of the many times when all the military and police academy education kicks in. It is for this reason that Valery will only recommend professional people.

'One of my clients hired a twenty-, twenty-one-year-old kid in Nice. The kid learned the code for my client's safe, and got €1.7m out. He was arrested forty-five minutes later at the airport!'

Valery does not have any patience for this kind of amateurish display, or for such a betrayal of a client's trust. It is taking a foolish risk too.

'Certain people, if you steal from them, you will disappear for years. Or forever.'

In the past Valery has been entrusted with transporting a *huge* amount of cash on some occasions. He uses huge bags to carry cash. 'Like when you are moving house. I worked in Hatton Garden. There are *so many* illegal operations there, mainly in diamonds and gold. I was trusted to carry pure gold sand. Pure gold sand is *very* heavy. My wrists were handcuffed to the bags, and the bags weighed up to forty kilos. You can't run with it!'

Valery continued: 'Hatton Garden is like spiders in a tank eating each other. All diamonds these days are *tagged,* so a diamond comes up as stolen immediately. This goes *especially* for the rare diamonds, like The Spirit of the Rose diamond which sold for $26.6m in 2020.'

Valery will not go near any client who is involved in illegal narcotics.

As he put it, 'Drug cartels have unlimited money. They have 50 mm machine guns which can go through your bulletproof car.

'I can't guarantee my client's safety if he is dealing with drugs'.

In fact, Valery says no not just to clients using drugs, but to sex trafficking, paedophiles, private military campaigns, drug trafficking and prostitutes. Other people in his network aren't quite so choosy though.

'One guy I know swallowed 2.1 kg of drugs for £100,000.'

When he does find clients he wants to work with – as with Josh, Piotr, Ejeneca, Brett and Walrus – Valery has become very close to some of them and some of their families. Overseas, Valery has done some royal family protection work. Not the British royal family, though, he hastens to add. 'They *only* use SAS and British police.'

As Valery said: 'When a customer pays you a lot of money you create a bond. £2k to £5k a week creates a bond, you become part of the family. There is one global client who lives in London. I know when he gets up, when he visits a prostitute, that his wife has a drinking problem... I know it all.'

This closeness while working for the client does not mean these intimate relationships last forever. Relationships can end when the contract ends. Sometimes they end because, with volatile financial and political circumstances, the client goes bankrupt.

Valery puts the corruption he sees succinctly: 'London is the European wallet.'

This has certainly been exposed by the Russian/Ukraine conflict and the murky paper trails tracing back to Russian oligarch wealth.

With Valery around you learn more fundamental things too, like watching your personal belongings. 'I knew a guy who had two guys come up to him in the street and tap his wrist. He didn't realise that they took his £275k limited edition watch.'

At their first meeting Valery told Emma off for having her handbag open with her iPhone visible!

Valery's vast experience has granted him a unique perspective on the spectrum and work and hazards close protection can expose you to, and the different skills you need to bring. 'It depends what industry your client works in. Sometimes basic stuff protects. At the highest level of threat though – so think Afghanistan, Middle East. For that preparation just in the UK before you go takes two or three weeks. You are carefully planning primary and secondary routes. You are analysing the political situation. Is there a civil war?

'It is best to work with local special operations, for example when you go to Morocco. You get someone who knows the country. Tactical, physical and guns training isn't enough with a country you have no knowledge about. You need to conduct a proper risk analysis. Your physical appearance and tactical knowledge will not be enough. If your client is targeted, you pretty much need an army of trained killers. You need a private military campaign.'

## Chapter 7

# RIK

**'From a young age I always knew I was a protector. I was bullied at school. I didn't want people to feel what I felt. I joined the army and moved into close protection.'**

Ivan Stevens was responsible for introducing us to another one of his extraordinary young charges too, Rik, a charming surveillance expert. Rik has experience of everything from exposing serial infidelity to busting corrupt gangs ripping off big corporations.

Ivan's protégé Rik has worked for a colourful range of private clients, doing work that he describes in his cheerful, attractive northern accent.

'Yeah, I've done '"grab and bag" interrogation. That sounds bad, doesn't it?!'

Put simply, 'Grab and bag' is using surprise to apprehend

a target for interrogation by throwing a bag or other disorientating covering over their head. Its intention is to catch the person off-guard, to unnerve them, and to conceal the journey they are being taken on for the interrogation, as well as the destination.

Rik continued: 'The surveillance industry is very diverse. I did a lot with the county line drug gangs in Shropshire. That was surveillance of massive gangs that led to arrests. In close protection I've worked in everything from replacing people to pick up a parcel to working with billionaires. It's like being back in the military. It's like a big family. It is all based on family values.'

Rik's friendly, casual demeanour and, the first time we met, Superdry navy and silver fleece, conceal a truly steely and hyper-competent individual.

'My trainers told me I would go far. That's because I *do* give a fuck.

'I love what I do, it means so much to me. I bring passion, energy. It started with the training: that was when I knew. I've never been a classroom person at all. My first job I was all nervous excitement. People say, "Go in and chill." But I hate having time off!'

Rik's story is sometimes a tough one to listen to, but it has moulded him into a gifted and committed bodyguard. His background is from Sierra Leone. At our first meeting he wore dark-rimmed glasses, dark stubble, and he was friendly, open and very handsome.

From the very beginning, Rik's life was tough. He was fostered from eighteen months of age. 'Mum died a few years ago, Dad is still alive. I was sexually and physically abused as a child. My birth mum ran away from my birth dad, and then I was fostered by a family. On the eighth of the eighth eighty-eight I was adopted, when I was five. We always lived in the same house in Middlesbrough. Mum and Dad always kept the same landline. Dad worked offshore.'

His mum and birth mum kept in contact with each other. When Rik came back from Iraq in 2003, his mum handed him a number. It was his birth mum's. His youngest sister was also adopted into the family. They were brought up with old-school manners. 'Grandad was an old-school Irishman. He believed in discipline with the hand and the belt.'

Rik was bullied at school from an early age and in his view this is a key part of why he is who he is. He wanted to fight back but didn't want to… People circled around and did nothing while he was being punched, kicked and spat at. Once back in his home, he took his emotions out on the house, punching walls and doors.

After these negative formative experiences, Rik joined the army 'to protect people. The biggest protection you can do is in the army.'

Upon leaving the army his mum suggested security work, bodyguard work, she knew who he was as a person. He's done plumbing and electrical work but his mum intuited where his heart, and his gifts, truly lay. Now Rik's got a successful career, a happy marriage, some stability at last.

He joined the army in March 2001, the Royal Engineers at Bassingbourn Barracks. As part of his military training, each troop was set in competition with another, different troop. He started to learn the value of working as a unit in many different ways.

Rik didn't have any confidence when he joined the army. He was being open about his insecurities. It was a self-protection mechanism he had learned over years of abuse, to put himself down before somebody else did.

Basic training showed him how strong his mind was, though, and taught him self-respect. 'It was one of the first times I felt proud.'

In the army you have *structure*, and he needs structure. 'Nothing gives me more satisfaction than making sure someone has got back and they're safe. I'm not corporate at all. Why wouldn't you want a human connection with someone whose safety is in our hands? It is safety when we are in the line of fire.'

He *has* advised other people to go into it, too, because it has enriched his own life so much.

'The military, your professional life, it has to be in *you*. To be a soldier you have to be empathetic. You have to care about the people around you. I'm not a hero, but it would give me fulfilment to know I had given my life for somebody else. There is a unique brotherhood in the army.

I went to Germany and did the rest of my army career there. I did the 432 armoured licence. [The FV432 Armoured Personnel Carrier is a British Army tank] I went to Canada for two months, trained there, and then I went to Poland in exercises.'

Rik has taken lessons from many different people and different places.

'Iraq was eye-opening. It was *inspiring* to be in a war-torn country. You appreciate everything at home you take for granted. I gained a lot of knowledge from the Iraqi people. You don't need materialistic shit. It is true life in the Third World. They have love and they have empathy. They are both more connected and more disconnected. We're all connected...we're all balls of energy.'

His tour of Iraq made Rik feel that he had been 'brainwashed' at home. The soldiers had 'anthrax injections' before Iraq, it was compulsory. Rik knew 'people who got really ill, some even died from it. They had blood clots, DVT. NAPS are biological and chemical warfare. They're on the end of the table, malaria tablets too. Unlabelled in a little plastic tray.'

Rik was talking about the Nerve Agent Pre-Treatment Sets (NAPS) issued for protection against nerve agents such as Sarin or VX. Rik was very unnerved by what felt to him like live clinical trials being performed on soldiers.

Other aspects of army life, however, made much more sense to Rik.

'You're not shouted and screamed at because they're dicks in the army; it's because your actions could have killed somebody. Army guys know how to be manipulative, we can read people within a few minutes, we get to know what people's triggers are. I *have* used it in a bad way in the past. I have now apologised to those people. Narcissists are the easiest people to read. If you question a narcissist, you open end your questions. They *hate* that. My wife has massive amounts of empathy. They are the hardest to read. Their brain shuts down and becomes very submissive. A narcissist will fight, someone empathetic will flight.'

After leaving the army, his first CP course was in 2005. Rik retrained for his bodyguard course with Paradigm Security Solutions (PSS) under Robert Paxman in Shropshire.

Robert Paxman was Prince Harry's bodyguard in Afghanistan and is a close protection legend. A former SAS close protection instructor, he has over two decades' experience in threat mitigation and risk management. Like Rik, and so many others, Robert had served in the British Army and then, after that world-class training, worked and taught for years in high-threat environments globally, including managing operations for a client with more than 1000 security personnel in Iraq.

At Paradigm Robert has built up an extraordinary group of individuals like Rik who can conduct highly sensitive security operations on the basis of their quality training. All too familiar with the toll that this kind of heroic activity can take on mental health, Robert Paxman is also very involved in a charity, Talking2Minds, which assists sufferers of severe conditions such as post-traumatic stress disorder (PTSD). Robert himself had suffered chronic symptoms such as flashbacks and bad dreams which led to depression and a marital breakdown. This experience all fed into the superb training, physical and mental, that Rik received.

The core of Rik's training was a sixteen-day course in Whitchurch, near Shrewsbury in Shropshire.

After the theoretical work, which laid the necessary foundations of learning, they were put out on the ground doing practical work. They had a principal to work with on an industrial estate. They spent a lot of time just looking at how a team works and walks. They would get people to run in, take pictures and so on, so they grew accustomed to dealing with that kind of threat from members of the public or journalists.

When it came to the vehicle drills, the same formula applied: in the classroom then practical. The second course was mainly tactical drills and foot drills. They were taught about box formation with a one/two/three/four/five man team. Examples were shown on Powerpoint and, once learned, they were deployed in the field.

One exercise stood out for Rik. They had a rug to put toy cars on 'like when you were a kid. That was a good icebreaker for the driving techniques training!'

As Rik observed: 'I questioned a lot on my course.

I'm not an alpha male at all but I will sit back like a silverback. I will analyse everything, look at it, think about it. I can be an all-singing, all-swinging dick. A lot of people in the security industry want to be that. I manipulate people by, for example, throwing in the word "fuck" now and then, to disarm people. I don't want to bring someone in who is not going to fit. I will utilise people in the right way.'

As another part of their training, they had to do an essay on someone who had been assassinated. Rik did Gianni Versace, and really enjoyed getting under the skin of a notorious case like that. 'What happened? What went wrong? How would you mitigate it? How do you gain intelligence? We learn from our mistakes to make us better CP operatives. It was a spurned lover of Versace. Most assassinations around the world happen in the moment.'

Gianni Versace was shot and killed on the front steps of his mansion in Miami Beach, Florida on 15 July 1997. The assailant was twenty-seven-year-old serial killer Andrew Cunanan. Cunanan had already murdered four other people, and was one of America's most wanted fugitives from justice, before he travelled to Miami and took up residence at the Normandy Plaza Hotel for almost two months. The hotel was just a few miles from Versace's coastal mansion. A hotel staff member noted that Cunanan paid in cash and frequently changed his appearance to conceal his identity. He had met Versace in San Francisco years earlier.

When he shot Versace dead, a witness and police pursued

Cunanan but did not manage to catch him. The killer had fired at point-blank range, shooting the designer twice in the back of the head. Versace was only fifty years old. Cunanan shot himself dead a week or so later as the investigation closed in around him.

Versace's former partner Antonio D'Amico later told the press that Versace's family had urged him to hire bodyguards and extra security but as he thought that paparazzi shots of celebrities with giant bodyguards looked ridiculous and just drew more attention to themselves, he did not think that he needed them. Whether better close protection would have led to a different outcome on that tragic summer day we will never know, but these days it is taught as a cautionary tale to trained bodyguards like Rik.

Rik was very clear to us on the value of proper surveillance training, too.

'I did surveillance as part of my bodyguard course because it makes you more *vigilant*. The full surveillance course is massively important because it makes you *hyperaware*. We did live targets: we did the county lines drug gangs in Shropshire, we got documents on them, we did surveillance on meet-up, and large targets. We got quite a lot of intel that was used in the conviction of that gang.'

Certainly, this form of crime-busting is a force for good. The county lines drug gangs are notorious for exploiting very young children, sometimes as young as thirteen or fourteen, to follow their orders and effectively provide human shields to the older, more experienced gang members. These hardened criminals know that when the police use undercover cops and double agents they can't employ young teens, so these kids are recruited and exploited.

After a difficult childhood, it might not be reading too much into it to think that Rik could see himself in some of these young kids. He used surveillance to try to break the gang's stranglehold on some Shropshire communities.

Soon enough, Rik was able to apply all this knowledge and training on real, paid jobs, and he quickly built up an interesting client base. He worked for *OK!* magazine doing celebrity weddings. After that it was another big change when he worked offshore on oil rigs. Then he was doing close protection for England football players, celebrities, Hollywood stars. You're only as good as your last job… but Rik made sure that all his jobs were a success.

Rik shared the story with us of one surveillance job that sounded fairly routine when he was commissioned, but ended up as absolutely anything but ordinary.

The basic situation was that there was a London gang scamming Sony out of computer equipment. They were stuffing boxes full of worthless paper that were meant to be full of computer gear. As Rik put it: 'Surveillance had guys on Kensington High Street in all sorts of different vehicles. Vauxhall Astra vans, a motorbike, a taxi. They were all getting photos and other evidence for the police for two days.'

Rik's team tried a sting. How does that work?

'You get evidence of the drop and then snatch them at the van. We had an interrogator come with us. We watched the gang wipe the car down, which seemed weird. I planned to snatch both the guys we had under surveillance. I wanted to split the two of them up and interrogate them separately.

'We put a tracker on the car. I jumped out of the taxi we were in and put a tracker on again, and I found a new address for them. I said "Why don't we do them again tomorrow to see if they would do another drop?" How ballsy were they?'

He ran it through his team leader and Sony, and they agreed. They scoped the second sting site meticulously and spent two hours there getting a sense of what was going on. This level of surveillance takes real time and patience.

'We looked for scouts, and took pictures of them. They came, did the drop. My team grabbed a guy we had been watching.'

"It's not me you want, it's them you want!" the guy protested.'

Rik's colleague got hold of him. He was breathless and very stressed out.

'I need you here, Rik, I'm burnt now, he knows who I am!'

Rik leapt into action and went after the ringleader who had blown his friend's cover.

Rik chased him all through Paddington, his chest burning

he ran so far in pursuit of this guy, through packed streets with pedestrians jumping out of the way in shock.

With his last ounce of strength, Rik rugby-tackled him right outside the station.

The criminal said, 'The gig's up. Who are you? The police?'

Rik thought, 'We aren't the police, we can't arrest you, why aren't you running to the Tube? Make a scene, get yourself out of there! But he just sat there. It was weird.'

This high-speed apprehension was nevertheless an integral part of busting the gang and delivering a result for Sony, the client.

As another part of his corporate surveillance work, Rik has followed trucks carrying 'sensitive material'. These sensitive materials can have *three* layers of cordons, in case anyone gets through the first two cordons.

Rik has a funny story about one of these gigs, when the 'sensitive material' was a load of new iPhones worth £4 million.

'We were in a vehicle following the truck, within ten miles behind. We had a forward vehicle about five miles in front. In other words we had quite a lot of cover for the wagon.

'We kept seeing a Range Rover. It would go in front of the lead vehicle, it kept stopping at service stations.'

It was making everyone on that job really jumpy. It was such irregular behaviour. Rik explained: 'I said, "Something's not right, we need to go to Plan B", but it turned out it was just a woman who had IBS! She had to keep stopping at service stations. You couldn't make that shit up, pardon the pun. We had been worried they were going to get done over. We almost called for back-up as well! Our gaffer wanted to know what happened and why it de-escalated. I was so embarrassed having to explain to him.'

Rik certainly sees a diverse range of activity in his line of work. On another occasion when Emma spoke to Rik, he was watching a woman being threatened over a Bitcoin deal gone wrong. For Rik, lower-level surveillance like this is primarily about gaining intel on people's routines.

'I could write a book on infidelity. A lot of work I've done has been on the female side.'

Rik noted an intriguing gender difference in infidelity surveillance.

'Women are 100 per cent right when they suspect men of infidelity. Men are only 75 per cent to 90 per cent right when they suspect women... I have a duty of care to the people that are looking for that work. Men can over-analyse things because of their own insecurity. Sometimes you have to give home truths to people and tell them, "Shut the fuck up".'

Rik does asset protection other than protecting people too, though, as we have seen from his work protecting oil rigs, Sony equipment or sensitive materials in trucks. He has also been working on HS2. HS2 involves complex work looking after everything from heavy plant equipment, to construction workers, to the land, and even the protesters themselves.

Rik described the different challenges on HS2. 'With CP, when you are with a person day to day, you know what you are doing. If they're a celebrity they will have fans, but an asset like HS2 is *very* dynamic. You don't know what will happen. With protests, roadblocks, everything is very unpredictable. The protestors are often highly trained by military people. They've learned survival skills, construction skills, for example how to tunnel. You are looking after the protestors' welfare and wellbeing.'

Rik sees many of the same principles behind the protestors as you might witness with a thief trying to steal from a bank.

'They will protest but in the background they are behind you, flanking you.' On one occasion, the security team that Rik was on had taken the crowbars off some protestors because they posed a dangerous threat.

'The protestors turned the truth. On Facebook Live they claimed it was the security people waving crowbars. I ask loudly if they want a warm drink when they are filming us, I try to show we are being mindful of their welfare, not threatening them. They want it to look like negative footage. Protestors on HS2 land are your responsibility as security. If something goes wrong then HS2 or the government can get sued.'

Rik tried to take control of the site action using some of the psychological skills he learned in the army and at Paradigm.

'It is unexpected if you don't rise to it and you are not a

dickhead. They film you on their camera phones, they try to film you, for example, saying you understand about how bad it is that all the trees are being cut down. The "war camp", the protestors' headquarters, is *incredibly* elaborate. It's got log cabins, UPVC windows, a learning centre.

'A lot of them are rich kids who manipulate the weak. They use the not very intelligent people to be a roadblock. They are the vulnerable ones put at risk of being arrested.'

As with so much of the rest of his story, Rik is always alert to the underdog, to injustice. Protecting the weak from the strong is a defining part of who he is as a bodyguard.

## Chapter 8

# IVAN

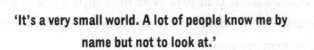

**'It's a very small world. A lot of people know me by name but not to look at.'**

Not many people know the British close protection world better than Ivan Stevens.

Emma arranged a meeting with Ivan Stevens and Laurie Black (more about him in chapter 9) in early October 2020 after several conversations with Ivan to gain his trust. Ivan has known Josh for thirty years, and that was how the connection first came about. His son, Carl, is a talented professional motorbike racer. Ivan now often sends Emma clips of him so she can watch him on TV. Ivan is a stocky septuagenarian who still does weights every day and looks at least twenty-five years younger than he is. His handshake is bone-crushingly firm.

Running teams of close protection for many years for a multitude of different principals and assets, Ivan chooses his associates with great care and always a degree of his trademark humour: 'A twelve-hour shift feels like a week if you work with an imbecile.'

It is the redoubtable Ivan Stevens running the massive security job at HS2 that Rik has been assigned to. As always the call came through the network: people come to Ivan. For Ivan to have 50 people on a team at HS2 he needs 75 people on the books. Because of the way shifts work they are doing 12-hour days: 84 hours a week. Some do two weeks of that, some do three. Ivan pays more than anyone else to get the quality and commitment that he needs. On HS2 he always has them in a minimum of teams of two.

As Ivan explained: 'You need ex-military. People from a civilian background would last about an hour. My teams get golf balls and ball bearings thrown at them, and bags of urine.'

When Emma spoke to Ivan on one occasion, there had been trouble at HS2.

'Five security guys got dragged out and had the crap beaten out of them.'

Even though Ivan insists that all of his people are ex-military, it's hard to prepare for something like this. Despite this, getting a place on Ivan's team is competitive. He had 105 people send him CVs and he ended up picking just twenty-seven of them. This is for a gig where amongst the things you routinely encounter protecting the asset are people 'firing golf balls at you from catapults and throwing stones'.

Ivan had his 'top blokes at COP26 on £300 a day. The higher surveillance people I was using for that are now doing stuff in Ukraine which will change a government.' Ivan's networks are second to none.

One story which tells you everything you need to know about Ivan dates from May 2021, when he was riding his scooter down the Old Kent Road late at night. He messaged Emma:

'Got attacked last night on the Old Kent Road two guys trying to steal my bike, needless to say they got more than they were expecting. Just think it's really bad that you can't drive on a major route in London without having to worry about someone trying to steal your possessions.'

Emma responded:

'That's absolutely horrendous. Are you OK? I bet they're not. And richly deserved.'

Emma had bet right.

'Small cut and a couple of bruises. I'm not sure but the first one might have a broken nose, police seemed amazed they didn't get my scooter.'

Ivan went on to express scepticism that the police would ever catch his assailants:

'No chance. A sad indictment of our country today that in our capital city this happens on a daily basis.

By his attitude he had done this often, I think I was the first one to fight back. He was totally shocked.'

Ivan was correct in that the police never tracked down his attackers, but there are two guys somewhere, one with a damaged nose, who might think twice about attacking an older man for his scooter. They certainly picked the wrong man in Ivan.

Ivan has a long view of how the British bodyguarding industry has changed, and according to him 'everything in security is about money now.'

In the past, his private clients have included some of the world's biggest celebrities.

'I did twenty-three hours without sleep doing security with Michael Jackson. We were subcontracted to a firm up north and there was a lot of rumour. The Sultan of Brunei had paid Michael Jackson £5 million just to turn up at his son's birthday, not even to perform. The venue was Stapleford Hall: a fifteenth-century property with a golf course attached. It is a *very* posh hotel. It was the best I have ever been looked after on any job. The food was amazing.'

He continued: 'Jerry Hall was there, Michael Jackson, Raquel Welch, Dionne Warwick, Don Johnson. This was the 1990s. The Sultan of Brunei had ten ex-SAS and fourteen Gurkhas protecting him! The Sultan's wife came in a brand-new Rolls-Royce which was apparently bulletproof. It's "hearsay" but we were told that Don Johnson and Jerry Hall disappeared together. The journalists didn't manage to get any pictures of MJ…'

How did Ivan reach the point of carrying out bodyguard work on glittering occasions like this?

Ivan's career started out as a favour for a fabulously wealthy friend running a nightclub, who, he told us, 'used to buy flash cars to woo the ladies. His name was James Lane and he made his money when he sold Mecca and bought Crockfords. This was 1979. James Lane had a club, and he didn't want the usual six-foot bouncer with cauliflower ears. The place was exclusive, and he used it for his private entertaining.'

Ivan was given a penthouse flat. Working the club, Bibas in Bromley, he was on the door from 9 p.m to 2.30 a.m. He only broke up two fights in two years there. Very sadly, Covid sent it into receivership after all those years.

Ivan's gift is, he said, 'I can talk virtually anybody down. Whatever you do, you are always looked on as the villain of the piece. When I left after two years…my phone hasn't stopped ringing since then. It is rare but when things go wrong you have to cuff someone and put them in the back of the van. Once someone was spitting and I pushed his head on his chest. I would go into a venue and say, "It's going to be one of those nights." You only have to look at the people going in to know.'

Ivan had an important point to make about high-profile

principals, one which also applies to the fictional relationship between David Budd and Julia Montague in *Bodyguard*. With very famous private clients, 'You cannot be starstruck, because you have to push back on VIPs if they are doing something dangerous. At a Boyzone concert I told someone to take their seat and it was Prince Harry!'

There's another reason why such perks of the job such as meeting celebrities can't be overly focused on: blackmail.

Ivan cautions that if you become obsessed with 'the experiences that come with the work then you've lost the credible edge and you get lost in showbiz or "red carpet fever" as we call it... If you lose focus you're open to all sorts of problems such as emotional or financial blackmail and manipulation and you can't do the job properly.'

Armed police officer Chris, coming at things from a different angle, entirely agreed with Ivan's point. 'It's *really* interesting work, the things you get to do, the people you see, it's remarkable, but if you are desperate to be a close protection officer you are probably not right. You can't be a "famous-loving person" – you have to be a steady Eddie character, unflappable. Only one or two people a year get to do it.'

## Chapter 9

# LAURIE

'With principals sometimes you have to be firm. With the royals, they are brought up with it, they accept it and they are usually easy to deal with. With private security, using close protection can be more of a status thing and they can be difficult.'

Ivan's contact and great friend Laurie Black has special forces links, and did close protection with Mohamed Al-Fayed. Particularly in comparison to chatty and clubbable Ivan, Laurie is reserved, even shy, but also has presence and gravitas. Ivan and Laurie met at the events arena in Battersea Park when they were both working there.

The first meeting with us took place on a cold but sunny day in Battersea, in the Park Police conference centre. Ivan and Laurie have known each other for almost twenty years, and have had a number of what Ivan calls 'set-tos' together.

Ivan opened the conversation by telling us that you can't be trained to be a bodyguard.

'It's just experience, you get a feeling. I always knew when Laurie was in trouble.'

Amongst the many interesting things that he has done, Laurie is involved in the final exercise for police training, giving him a unique perspective that he was happy to share.

'The training is for people who become Royal Military Police, Royal Marines, Royal Airforce Police. RaSP [Royalty and Specialist Protection] too: the TV bodyguard was in that.'

Laurie is right. In real life David Budd might well have been on his police training exercise, as a future principal protection officer (PPO) in RaSP.

Laurie continued to tell us about the training. It is a twelve-week course and he is involved in the final week. It is incredibly demanding and would need someone with David Budd's stamina and determination to succeed.

'There is a 70 per cent failure rate on the course. You have to be very good with weapons. You have to be very fit. You have to blend in.'

Part of Laurie's role is to set up an area and a scenario with the instructors. The trainees come into Battersea Park and he has someone hidden in the bushes with weapons. They hit the team with fake bullets and the objective is that they have to get the VIP through.

'They are *exhausted* by this point in the course. They get attacked all over the place by different police officers. You can hear guns firing. "Gun shots in Battersea Park": Google it! For the 30 per cent who pass, their future main role is looking after senior British Army officers, VIPs, ambassadors. They go to Afghanistan, Lebanon, Khartoum. My friend has just retired as lieutenant colonel after thirty-three years.'

Laurie has even seen someone get sacked on the day in the very final exercise.

'An officer walked around. She stood in front of the gunman and it got her sacked. Usually you have an instinct about who can pass. It's roughly 90 per cent men, 10 per cent women on this training course. There are some *very* good female officers.'

Laurie and his wife have both on occasions acted as principals during the training exercises. Laurie jokes that his wife, Dana, was a better actor than him!

In the military they have a course, and then a two-day exercise. The military do not normally contact Laurie until the final week.

'In the final exercise it's 24/7. The guys are under pressure all the time, especially with the firearms exercises.' It is an important means of assessing whether they could handle such pressure in real life.

Laurie even got a deputy mayor as a principal.

'The deputy mayor was very pro-military and when he was on the course he absolutely loved it. His father was quite a famous soldier in World War II, Lieutenant-Colonel Norman Field. He was in charge of Churchill's Secret Army.'

All the principals that Laurie uses have to be military or ex-military. His training courses run through the year and all the course instructors are ex-military, too. Longmoor Military Camp, off the A3 road in Hampshire, is where their training exercise is held.

Laurie explained that when you are a principal with the military, after you have completed the training exercise, you are shown all the people who were surveillance: 'Tramps, street cleaners. It's very eye-opening. You have got to be exceptionally fit, and you must be able to shoot. Anyone can fail, including on the last day. Targets come up, and if you shoot civilians by accident, then you can fail. You can only try twice. The military don't explain what the points were that you failed on, either.'

We wanted to learn more about what had led Laurie to this interesting juncture in his impressive career. As for many of our CP contacts, it's in the blood with him.

He was born in Glasgow, and moved to Brighton with his dad in 1967. His dad was a CP officer with Sussex Police. Laurie's dad joined Special Branch in 1978, and in that role he looked after Harold Wilson. He had a heart attack around 1987 and retired on medical grounds.

Laurie left school at sixteen, worked in a Wimpy Bar until he was eighteen, and then he also joined Sussex Police.

After gaining experience there, he joined the Royal Military Police in 1980. He wanted to join the army but was unable to because his eyesight wasn't good enough.

He was posted to Germany, where he was tasked with policing the military. After that he spent four years in Northern Ireland, then he was posted to London, and did some trips with the then FCO (Foreign & Commonwealth Office).

Laurie also worked at Harrods for four years before he came to Park Police twenty-nine years ago. In that capacity he was employed by Wandsworth Council, which has a police force, and he's still there now. He's been policing parks and open spaces, including major events.

He and Ivan did the Battersea fireworks display together in November 2021: 'A hundred thousand people, and not one incident on our watch!'

Laurie certainly has some stories. 'When I was in the military doing weapons training, in those days you trained at Chichester. My first CP job was looking after injured soldiers at Royal Victoria Hospital in Belfast; they were in a secure ward, because they were under threat from IRA attacks. My father was an investigating officer in the Brighton bombing. You get time off after something like that...'

One of the real highlights of all these years for Laurie was when he did the Toronto Summit with Margaret Thatcher, providing vital aid to her dedicated personal team.

'The Toronto Summit I did, Thatcher and Reagan were

both there. We were looking after her hotel room, escorting her equipment, bags and so on.' There was a ring of steel required around these politicians, at the time the two most famous world leaders, with a profile and a potential threat level far above even David Budd's principal, Home Secretary Julia Montague.

'I was in Brussels with Thatcher too. Thatcher was great. She was appreciative and friendly. She didn't sleep very much, she was working a lot, and she was very polite. Denis wasn't there, we never met him, she travelled with her PA. I did not encounter any major threats, although I met someone in a bar who could have been a threat. The threat then was purely the IRA, and also animal rights people then were potentially very dangerous too.'

A firm hand can be required: 'With principals sometimes you have to be *firm*. With the royals, they are brought up with it, they accept it and they are usually easy to deal with. With private security, using close protection can be more of a status thing and they can be difficult. For example if you want to take a different route to the route you took yesterday they can be resistant.'

What changed the close protection world in Ivan and Laurie's view was the Security Industry Authority (SIA) coming in to regulate for the 2012 Olympics.

'Anyone could become a close protection officer. Now the money isn't good because so many people have become close protection officers. They have diluted what CP is now.

You can have people on £8 an hour wearing a CP badge. SIA was meant to regulate but made it worse.'

Laurie pointed out: 'Prior to SIA CP badges, the CP circuit in London was quite small. It was called "the circuit". You would get calls, to look after someone like Elton John. I would get calls while I was in the old Harrods repository bar.

'You still have to do a course to get a CP badge but now it's only a two-week course. Ivan has never done the CP course. Excellentia, John Morrison's outfit, is the best CP training company. Their course is really hard.'

Given the choice, Laurie would not have left the Royal Military Police, he would have stayed. He didn't get the choice though. He was very seriously injured in Northern Ireland during a riot. He got a pavement slab dropped on his head, which is why his memory is not so good these days. It was 31 August 1983. He was out and 'expecting trouble' on foot patrol, in the middle of a West Belfast housing estate. Then he was knocked out. He came to after a couple of minutes with someone trying to pull his rifle off him. His comrades dragged him into the back of a vehicle and he was hospitalised for three weeks. The slab damaged the frontal lobe of his brain. He gets a war pension now. Despite the lifelong effects of his injury, he has been promoted to inspector now. 'I am pretty lucky as a CP officer.'

Between 1988 and 1992 Laurie was making a cool £40,000 a year working with Mohamed Al-Fayed, but the cash was hard-earned with that demanding client.

'It was great money. The director at the time was a retired major, he said to me, "Do you want a job?" I met Dodi a few times, but Diana wasn't on the scene yet. At Harrods I started in uniformed security. Then I went on to one of the teams looking after Mohamed Al-Fayed himself.

'He lived in Park Lane. You had to wear a different coloured shirt every day to prove that you weren't "dirty" and wearing the same shirt two days running! Al-Fayed was "quirky" to put it mildly. A couple of guys left Harrods to take a big pay cut and go back to the army because ultimately work in the military suited them better.'

Both Ivan and Laurie believe that with this particular client base, the Arab community and the 80 per cent of billionaires with London residences, CP work is about status rather than a real threat, and it was all about status with Al-Fayed. After that experience, Laurie values all the upsides of his present role at Battersea.

## Chapter 10

# TERRORISM

Laurie's very personal experience during the Troubles in Northern Ireland, and his description of the threats facing world leaders such as Thatcher and Reagan in the 1980s, got us thinking about more recent terrorist threats, notably those that have involved CPs and AFOs (authorised firearms officers) in the UK.

The 11 September 2001 terrorist attacks changed the world as we know it. Under new guidelines, codenamed Operation Kratos, more forceful methods were laid out for identifying, confronting and containing the threat from suspected suicide bombers and terrorists. Coming from a society where police firearms training always encourages the use of firearms to remove the threat rather than kill, this was a very radical, and highly controversial, paradigm shift.

A 2005 briefing note headed 'Counter Suicide Terrorism' from the Metropolitan Police Service (MPS) to all members put it in these bald terms:

> Following the discussions at full Authority on 28 July I now attach a briefing note prepared by the MPS on the tactics to be deployed in the event of an armed encounter with suspected suicide bombers. This is a national policy which was adopted by ACPO [Association of Chief Police Officers] centrally and ratified in 2003. It's known as Operation Kratos. 'Shoot to kill' is a vernacular term which the police themselves prefer not to use.

With, at this point in history, very limited experience of suicide bombings on British soil, Operation Kratos had to seek guidance from countries with the misfortune to have a better first-hand understanding of it, including Sri Lanka and Israel.

The guidelines state that when it is clear a suspected suicide bomber has no intention of surrendering, the head or lower limbs should be aimed at. The normal target, the torso, is highly inadvisable in this specific case as it is the region most likely to trigger detonation of a suicide belt if fired at. The same goes for Taser use.

The 2005 MPS briefing concluded:

Operation Kratos is the policing tactic for person borne suicide terrorism. National policy ratified by ACPO TAM. Under the command of specially trained designated senior officer. 3 stages as per SOP Officers deployed covertly to give the element of surprise – if challenged will detonate. 2 options: 1. If 100% sure head Shot 2. If not sure, challenge from a position of safety. Officers to react dependent upon the suspect's reaction – in accordance with their training from the ACPO firearms manual of guidance. Reason for head shot: 1. Peroxide explosives very volatile. If fired at, hit or tasered WILL Detonate. 2. Need for immediate incapacitation to prevent person detonating device.

For the last two decades, close protection officers have had to have a deep familiarity with Operation Kratos guidelines, in order to be able to protect those they serve in the event of a suicide attack.

It would not be long before, tragically, Operation Kratos guidelines had to be put into action.

A truly dreadful attack took place on 22 March 2017 in Westminster, when fifty-two-year-old terrorist Khalid Masood killed a policeman, PC Keith Palmer, and four others. Masood seriously injured another twenty-nine people. He had ploughed through pedestrians on Westminster Bridge before fatally stabbing PC Palmer, who was guarding the 'weak', vulnerable security point at the Carriage Gates.

A real-life example of how close protection counter-terrorism training kicks in was, unfortunately, provided by these Westminster Bridge terror attacks. During this terrorist incident, it was a quick-thinking protection officer, working for the defence secretary, who shot Masood dead. This protection officer was part of the Royalty and Specialist Protection branch of the Metropolitan Police, which as we have seen plays a vital role in protecting royalty and major political figures.

The two close protection officers who found themselves most closely embroiled in the terrible event had started their day's work at Lambeth headquarters. They then moved to a second location, the Palace of Westminster, where, at the start of their shift, they were to meet the principal they were responsible for. So far, a standard day for these brave, highly trained officers.

At the inquest, the jury were played CCTV footage of both officers running through New Palace Yard towards the incident, just moments after the fatal stabbing of PC Palmer by Masood. The whole event took just eighty-two seconds. The officers heard the 'explosion' of Masood's car crash, and noticed uniformed police officers shouting and waving their batons. Decisive, lethal force was required.

Thanks to their swift actions, the terrible death count was not even higher, but even so, in addition to PC Palmer, four other people lost their lives as a result of the attack: Aysha Frade (44), Leslie Rhodes (75), Kurt Cochran

(54) and Andreea Cristea (31). Cristeea, who fell off the bridge after being injured in the attack, succumbed to her injuries two weeks later; the other three died on Westminster Bridge.

Both police officers were granted anonymity at Masood's inquest and they gave extraordinarily dramatic and moving evidence beneath the public gallery in Court One of the Old Bailey. The officers, codenamed SA74 and SB73 under condition of the anonymity they had been granted, were able to demonstrate that they followed protocol.

On the footage shown to the jury, both officers could be seen, arms outstretched, holding their guns, shouting at Masood to try to dissuade him from his lethal actions.

Hugo Keith, QC, the coroner for the Metropolitan Police, suggested to SA74 he had no option but to shoot to prevent Masood killing him and others. The QC could see from the footage that SA74 moved backwards in order to give the assailant time to stop before he opened fire. However, Masood continued the advance on SA74 with murderous intent, and a point was reached where he was close enough to have killed the armed officer, had he not opened fire. There was also, of course, a real risk that Masood might have a bomb or be wearing a suicide vest.

SA74's words were powerful.

'I did not know what was happening but I was certain that something terrible was happening. I saw a large black male running purposefully towards me. He was carrying two large knives and I could clearly see that they were covered in blood. He was going to kill me.'

Without slowing down or changing pace, Mr Keith observed that SA74 did not even have time to aim carefully. SA74 attended to the wounded suspect after disabling the threat, and, though he could not be saved, tried to offer medical assistance. SB73 was also in attendance and performed CPR on the attacker, but he died of three gunshot wounds, two in the torso, from SA74's Glock pistol.

One of the other most notorious British terror attacks in recent years is of course the London Bridge attacks. It took place just a few months after the lethal attacks on Westminster Bridge, on 3 June 2017.

Three Islamic State terrorists went on a stabbing and killing spree around Borough Market on a busy night out. Footage of the terrible events shows that, despite the assumption that anyone would flee such a scene, many individuals froze, unable to process what was happening and make a run for it. Of course, it was AFOs who saved the day, but not before eight people had been killed and another forty-eight injured. The three attackers were shot dead by authorised firearms officers from both the Metropolitan Police and the City of London Police. The bravery of their actions was heightened by the fact that all three men were wearing explosive vests that were only confirmed to be fake when the threats had already been disabled.

Despite the swift, courageous and effective response to both the London Bridge and Westminster terror attacks, not everything about the system is nimble. The civilian authorities have to give authorisation before a military unit can be called into action in the event of a terrorist threat. COBRA is a crisis response committee that sits within Whitehall and is usually the source of such an authorisation; it is headed by a major government figure or the Prime Minister themself. It is COBRA's role to assess the threat level and decide the response.

There is a sense that terrorist attacks are rarely isolated incidents; rather they could be launched nationwide, possibly in several places simultaneously. This has placed pressure on the UK Police Federation to train hundreds more officers for counter-terrorism duties, but, as we have seen, training to the standard required takes a minimum of two years. It can't be done overnight, and many officers who volunteer for the training are ultimately not up to it.

The fact that there is a great deal of secrecy around exactly how many counter-terrorism officers there are is consequently a bit of a worry. Do we have enough in the event of a major attack? Is the figure being kept from the public (and the terrorist cells) because it isn't high enough?

## Chapter 11

# EJENECA

**'Issues rarely exist with a client. They exist mainly with the team, the people that you work with.'**

The fortune cookie Emma got the evening that she met Ejeneca said 'today you will meet someone who will become important to you'. Ejeneca and Emma had a good laugh about that, but it turned out to be the case. Ejeneca is a tough, pretty, hyper-vigilant ball of energy who peppers her conversation with hilarious anecdotes and copious swearing.

Ejeneca has an important mantra for how she deals with clients: 'Kiss arse but don't lick arse! These people are paying you because they trust you with their life and also with what you find out.'

When Ejeneca was considering her career choices, one of her oldest friends thought that close protection work would suit Ejeneca 'to a tee'. The friend remembers Ejeneca even in her early days sticking up for people, not being scared, and she stopped people being bullied. A disciplined person, she doesn't really drink and just smokes a bit. 'In my industry you can't be partying 24/7, so it suited my personal lifestyle.'

Ejeneca got into close protection by a series of pretty unusual routes. The immediate catalyst was a break-up of an eight-year relationship, but she had also looked into the army and police when she was younger. She started to research close protection. She educated herself. She watched videos on Google and booked a course. She found the written aspect the most challenging, but as far as the physical side of it: 'I 100 per cent loved it. I got an 83 per cent mark. I've always been very strong and athletic.'

During her first conversation with Emma, this feisty female bodyguard gave a very lively account of the varied jobs she had been swiftly asked to do after she completed her training. She keeps a list of all her jobs and shared it in confidence. To begin with: 'I did a lot of Jewish stuff. Festive events. I worked at a strip club for four weeks.'

In the end though, it was a Facebook ad that started her in close protection for real. She got her licence in January 2016 and her first CP contract in August 2016. She started with the most extraordinary first job, when she got picked to look after a princess from Bahrain. It was a six-week gig, with a teenage royal principal. Ejeneca doesn't work for her any more – 'They don't put you on a retainer!' – but she still sees them at hotels and so on.

Since then, Ejeneca's jobs have been incredibly varied. They range from big corporate gigs, like the Shell AGM, to a *Fear of the Walking Dead* screening, to a counter-terrorism surveillance job in Canary Wharf. Just before the first lockdown, Ejeneca worked for a prestige company doing close protection work. The job also involved driving eight McLarens around the UK.

After that she was in Hertfordshire for four months watching a supplier. She has done work at the security company employed by Victoria Beckham's firm. Ejeneca even spent part of 2021 doing Covid testing and security work at South Mimms.

She was booked into an AGM in late May 2021. That was remunerated at £250 for four or five hours' work. This is a good rate, which reflects the fact that they want a certain calibre of people there. She is campaigning for better pay because, as she said, 'People tend to keep quiet, and take what they are given to keep working. Once you have signed T&Cs and a confidentiality agreement, you are discouraged from discussing the rate.'

She also did *X Factor*, where she was part of a team in charge of looking after the judges and crowd control.

'Simon Cowell is an amazing guy, really, really nice, he takes the time to speak to people.

'Nine out of ten times you judge what's in front of you.

That becomes embedded in you as a habit. You have to keep your skills going. You can be put on a fire exit and you can still learn something from it. Someone at *X Factor* burst through a fire door. Suddenly there I was chasing a guy running for the Green Room. He got directly into the judges' rooms! Money, bags, jewellery, there was all sorts in there.

'You get paid the same whether you are at a fire door or in the crowd listening to shit for six hours.'

Ejeneca is a great believer in authenticity. 'Show a bit of your true self and maybe that's why I get the work that I get. As a child I used to say, "I want Action Man, I don't want Barbie!"'

We wanted to know what kind of jobs a client might prefer a woman for. As one juicy example, Ejeneca told us that early in her career she heard a rumour that a member of a royal family had 'done the dirty' with a bodyguard. 'They sacked all the male bodyguards and were looking for women!'

On another memorable occasion Ejeneca did a Burberry event in the middle of the forest covering people's positions: 90 per cent were male, there were just two girls, Ejeneca and one other. Some men took an extra thirty minutes' break. The two girls, on the other hand, didn't even take an extra five minutes. Ejeneca has made some good female friends in this job, and sometimes they definitely need to stick together.

'My client needs to be number one as well as my team.'

Ejeneca wants to retain the same team she has now, but

that is not possible. Why are they better than some more male-dominated teams she's worked for? 'It's the dick measuring competition...' When as a female bodyguard 'you go six hours without the toilet', it is not appealing to deal with male egos as well. 'With surveillance you do your own thing. In a team it's a different set-up, you have worked with these people before, and the money is better.'

Ejeneca has accumulated experience across a few different jobs now where she had a hybrid role with families: part driver, part close protection.

One of her drivers, Ibrahim, is a good mate to her now. He has been in the industry for ten years. Ejeneca enjoys driving, too and she is working towards the top driving qualification that can be achieved. Ejeneca started driving during one job, which was 'driving a yellow Lamborghini, it was just incredible!'

Happy in a relationship, unlike several of the other bodyguards we know, she wants a work/life balance these days, too. 'I want to stay in the security industry. My missus wants to open her own vegan coffee shop. I would do a business with her...'

In Ejeneca's view, sure there is competition in the industry but there is *more than enough* to go around. 'I love what I do. This industry is naughty though, people will trip you up, not offer you an open hand. But as with most industries this is the world now: be prepared, spot the signs, you will be OK!'

Ejeneca has dealt with some very peculiar client requests.

One female client, on a whim, made her buy 'thirty-six bottles of posh pink lemonade for £170.' Another client bought about £30,000 worth of chocolate in one day. Such private clients say: 'Ejeneca, it's hard for us to trust people.' They can't even trust their friends, because of the money. In her view and aspiration, she gives the people she looks after normality, and shows them another way of life, bridging cultural differences.

'The money is all a cover-up. They don't have *normality*.'

We wanted to know what her most lucrative gig has been. Her highest paid job was £400 a day, working for a sixteen-year-old girl. Concerned about the welfare of this client, she offered to help the girl in question run away. The girl said that they would both get killed if Ejeneca did that.

Ejeneca laid out what she believes are three different tiers of threat level with clients. 'When you're taking a client out, the majority don't have status where they are recognised here, unless it's royalty. With the heir to the throne of Bahrain her threat level is higher, but with my strip club lady and other clients who are not royalty, the threat is lower.

1. Critical threat: the sixteen-year-old girl. She had her watch and phone tracked, satellite tracking, she had a ransom on her head, she was changing vehicles every two days. 'She thought undercover tracking devices were normal. She didn't know!'

2. Status: people who just like to show that they can afford a bodyguard.
3. Companionship: people hire her simply because they want a bit of company.

If robbery is perceived as a particular threat, then certain clients want a bubble and a formation around them in Harrods and in Selfridges. They don't want to be touched. She takes her clients to different places depending on what they want to experience. For example, 'One Arab client loved the funfair'.

'What can I say about my clients? 50 per cent of the time I want to shoot myself, 50 per cent of the time I want them to extend their stay!'

She had serious adventures in the West End with a female client who wanted to party. It was just Ejeneca and a driver and the client gave a £2k tip to each of them for a seven day task. 'You don't do the job for the tip though. Some clients ask for 20p change! One guy won a million at a casino, he gave a random girl at the table a £20k chip. He literally threw the chip at her. He nearly fell on the floor, the bodyguard was holding onto the jacket because it was a £100k jacket. This guy got back at 3 a.m., and gave his bodyguard nothing, he just said I need you on shift at 9 a.m., as he had been the previous days!'

She has got really close to some families, including the 'nightclub girl' who still sends her amazing messages. That girl could have got her into serious hot water though. An Arabian female in her twenties, she went to a strip club and a nightclub with Ejeneca, and they smoked cigars. She was filming on her phone and Ejeneca had to stop her...

Ejeneca chain-smokes roll-ups as she describes these jobs, using very salty language with plenty of f-bombs. She ended our wonderfully entertaining first encounter with the question: 'So was it worth the wait?' Yes!

The most recent time Emma caught up in person with Ejeneca, she was on a high. She was working for £325 a day 07.00 to 17.00 with a Middle Eastern client based in Windsor and had been to Turkey and Abu Dhabi. Her high though, was that prior to that gig, she had been on such an extraordinary job with an A-list Hollywood couple and their two children that she felt she had been spoiled for any other bodyguard work. As Ejeneca pointed out, 'even their parents were amazing and said "we missed you"!' These A-listers had no nanny, so Ejeneca as their 'security driver and requisite bodyguard when I need to be' *was* their UK entourage. What was it like working with the female celebrity?

'She's a mum. She would say "girls we have to clean your shoes before you get in the car." They are normal people. I was never *told* to do anything, I was *asked*. They were respectful. They brought a teacher with them who has also taught Kanye and J Lo's kids. The girls loved me. They wrote me lovely letters and gave me little gifts.'

A key point of vigilance for Ejeneca was that the female celebrity has a lot of stalkers. 'Some have sent her gifts and even death threats.' This was something Ejeneca had been briefed to be aware of no matter how fun the job was. The couple find the paparazzi less oppressive in the UK than in the US, which they usually call home. Outside of his insane diet and gym routine the male celebrity was spending a lot of time filming in the Home Counties. The female was not away filming and very attentive to her daughters.

That is not to say they weren't a handful at times. Despite being one of the most famous leading men in Hollywood, her male client had a habit of wandering off. While his stunning wife was usually able to go incognito in hats, masks and sunglasses, the male was recognised even when trying to disguise himself. 'Maybe he should have worn bigger glasses and a different style hat!' Ejeneca would sometimes have to pick him up in the car in a frantic hurry because he had unilaterally decided to publicly meander around. She sympathised with this though, after all, 'he was just being normal, and sometimes forgetting who he is!'

At the Kensington Gardens Easter egg hunt, he was wandering about and got recognised, so Ejeneca had to intervene. She had to step in again when, leaving a theatre, her colleague was holding back the crowd surge effectively until the situation became overwhelming and she had to jump out of the car and take control. The male celebrity did not know the extent of the threat until he saw Ejeneca approach twenty people in ten minutes who posed a potential security risk. She was able to get them into the car and safely away but she hates situations like that.

Whether driving or on foot patrol, Ejeneca wants to be in control. It is this dedication and consummate professionalism that creates such strong bonds with the clients she is loyal to.

## Chapter 12

# THE VEHICLES

It is not just Ejeneca who emphasised the importance of vehicles and driving to us. Any close protection officer will tell you that vehicles are a key component of keeping their principals safe.

Armed response vehicles, commonly abbreviated to ARV, are a vital part of the British police armoury. An ARV carries weapons and ammunition. They also carry non-lethal weapons as part of addressing a spontaneous firearms incident. They are equipped to attend road crashes too. Amongst the sophisticated first aid equipment they carry is oxygen, blood and airway management and even an automatic defibrillator. They've got cones and signs, too, so they can secure a collision scene rapidly, as first responders.

It's one thing knowing what sort of kit is inside these ARVs. It's another hearing the crazy stories of how it gets used.

The cars our police officer contributor, Chris, describes have gun boxes. It's a massive box which carries carbines, bullets, stun grenades, smoke grenades. Then there's another box that has covert operations plans in it. They also carry ballistics shields. The kit takes up *a lot* of space. This means that they have to call another car to take the criminals away, which causes ill feeling, to put it mildly.

Chris was once in hot pursuit of a lorry and one of the officers in the vehicle with him threw a 'stinger' out. The Stinger Spike System uses strong steel spikes that can penetrate any tyre. The 'stinger' punctured the tyres and the criminal they were pursuing crashed and ran off. During this high-speed chase, Chris's vehicle got another call. They ended up chasing another lorry, and they went ahead, ready to do a stinger. It was the same guy!

They always carry one stinger in a car. An HGV takes up a lot of spikes, so you have to replace it once you've used it on a huge lorry, but miraculously on this occasion Chris had two stingers in the car! He had stung his second lorry within about half an hour.

They found £400k worth of stolen kit in the lorry. 'It was brilliant, really exciting,' Chris said. 'It takes *ages* to write up an incident like that but the teamwork is really good.'

As Chris put it: 'Everything we do in a firearms situation is *managed*, there is a *hierarchy*.' That hasn't prevented some bizarre incidents though.

Chris was called out in his vehicle to one firearms job.

It was really nasty. He arrived to find a couple of dead people in a house who had been murdered with a shotgun. They needed to scour the surrounding area for the killer. It was a busy scene in the countryside with loads of woods. Chris had received information that the suspect was in the trees. He was looking around, alone. Then he saw someone. He raised his gun. Then looked again. It was a *statue*!

Such jitters come from a place of genuine anxiety though. Sarah says of her husband: 'I fear for Chris, sometimes he is too brave for me. I'm always confused by whether I am really proud of him or really cross with him when he does brave things... He came home singed once. I don't worry about Chris on firearms jobs, I worry about him on road traffic jobs.'

On another occasion, Chris was called following reports of a car driving around pointing guns at people.

They tracked the car down and stopped it. They shouted: 'Armed police, show your hands!' In the end, there were five stops. 'One lad was sitting on the floor. Hands behind his head, an increasing dark patch on his trousers. He had wet himself! Those boys were driving around town with a toy gun thinking it was funny. It isn't so funny when you get armed response vehicles with *real* guns.'

Jonathan Hourihan learned all about the vehicles filming his Ross Kemp programme about the armed police. In the West Midlands they use a fleet of bulletproof Audis. In West Yorkshire they have some amazing Range Rovers and armoured military-type vehicles. In the City of London they educated Jonathan about their use of helicopters, motorbikes and CCTV. When the show interviewed a group of young gang members in Birmingham, they referred to the police as 'the biggest gang' and, after touring the country seeing their kit and capability, we can see they have a point.

Meanwhile in Devon and Cornwall, the armed police are also traffic cops, which is why it is not unusual down in Devon to see a traffic officer with a sidearm. If you see a police officer with a gun in Devon, Cornwall and Dorset that does not necessarily mean that a firearms situation is taking place, because as the Devon and Cornwall Police website says:

'Firearms officers have a standing authority to overtly carry a sidearm whilst on duty.

'They carry additional skills such as traffic policing, therefore will routinely assist at other incidents such as road traffic collisions (RTCs) and will also assist with general police duties as they are sworn constables.'

Devon, Cornwall and Dorset are known collectively as the Alliance. Officers are generally constables, sergeants and inspectors, but they can be male or female and they can be any age as long as they are capable of passing the fitness tests. Firearms officers do not receive higher remuneration than non-armed police officers, and they are all volunteers. Fortunately, the last shooting recorded by Alliance officers was in 2004.

The Initial Firearms Course for the Alliance is eleven

weeks, with refresher training throughout the year. Their preferred sidearm is the Glock 17 pistol. Whilst all firearms officers are trained to the same base role profile, some then choose to specialise in other areas such as rifle, close protection, dynamic entry, surveillance and command. Alliance officers can also work outside the three counties if they are required to be deployed for major events, such as the Olympics or the G8 Summit.

The aspired response time to an incident by Alliance officers is to attend all immediate incidents with fifteen minutes in urban locations and twenty minutes for rural locations. This can however be much faster depending on where the nearest police resource is at the time of the call.

Since the Metropolitan Police rolled out 600 new trained counter-terrorism officers in London and other units in big UK urban areas in 2016, they have enjoyed some of the most extraordinary kit. Their specially adapted BMW F800 motorcycles allow them to race to any major incident even in heavy traffic. The bikes are all-terrain and can reach a breath-taking top speed of 120 mph.

If an assault on water is required, for example in the event of piracy, the elite counter-terrorism police have rigid inflatable hull vessels. Their training and aircraft also allow them to abseil into terror incidents from helicopters. As a terrorist that's probably not what you would want to see bearing down on you.

For those ex-military and police private close protection officers, the vehicle might be a Rolls-Royce or an S-Class Mercedes. A royal protection officer might be driving a £300,000 Bentley on the job. That's not likely to resemble their own car! The purpose remains the same: protecting the public or the principal from harm.

In the US, Valery drove a Rolls-Royce luxury SUV. 'It's so quiet inside. It goes so smoothly. It's extremely expensive.' He was speeding once because the client asked him to. He was doing 110 miles an hour instead of 65. He got stopped and slapped with a $600 speeding ticket. Val protested. The police officer said: 'You're driving a half a million dollar vehicle.' You don't want to play with US police officers. His Chinese clients, on the other hand, tend to hire private drivers to drive their ultra-luxury cars, while most embassies Valery has worked with use S-Class Mercedes.

For an American bodyguard like Brett, whom we will meet later, his bodyguard kit has to include SUVs. Why?

'They sit up higher and we can see a crowd from a distance, and we can have pretty much of an upper hand on the crowd, we can dictate, and see people clearly. So, we do try to stay in the SUVs more than anything else.'

The unique line of sight they offer is critical in protecting the celebrities and VIPs that Brett and his team look after. This specific point about SUVs is just one part of the much wider, varied and totally essential role that vehicles play in close protection and bodyguard work.

## Chapter 13

# 'LUCKY' ANDY

**'You never run from anywhere. You hold your nerve and walk. You always need a cover story.'**

Andy Copley, known to his friends as 'Lucky' is, quite simply, one of the top surveillance people in the country. Ivan worked with him at a huge Battersea Park fireworks display and was so taken with his stories that he called Emma.

'You *need* to speak to Andy. If he is willing to tell you half of what he's told me... Some of the tools that he's got you would not believe. This guy is employed by multi-millionaires.'

Emma set it up. Speaking on a WhatsApp call for their first interview, Andy was charismatic, intriguing and alluring from the start.

His stories were outlandish, outrageous. Some of them

sounded like tall tales, and the characters Andy had under surveillance varied from sleazy, to dangerous, to plain sick. In all cases, Andy's tenacity and complete unwillingness to let a good trail go cold was always plain to see.

He sent Emma his CV, but she was keen to have him bring his experiences to life in his own words. As we wanted to know with all our cast members, how had he got into this business in the first place?

Andy started out, like many of our other cast members, in the army. He was still in the army when he did his police training. However, his first wife wanted him to leave the army, so he did. He joined a tactical team within the police, the anti-drugs team. He also spent time in the domestic violence team.

Also while he was in the police, Andy was a CROPs officer. CROP is an acronym for covert rural observation post. Whilst this surveillance specialism is generally conducted in rural surroundings, CROP work can also be utilised within an urban environment. The specialised skills for this intriguing art are learned in either military or police specialist covert operations units. Andy learned in the latter. As a CROPs officer, Andy did surveillance. In that capacity, he 'could do twenty-four hours impromptu, with sleeping bags and rations.'

He did surveillance on a well-known celebrity who had been caught up in the death of a member of the public.

Andy stayed in the celebrity's road to do the surveillance. It was a really hot day. Spending twelve hours in a van is a very hard routine. 'You have your invisible cloak on. There's a big roundabout [in the area] and they had gone there to go dogging or cottaging.

'There was a copse and I was hiding in it. [The celebrity] had his coat over his shoulder as a signal. At that point a kids' rugby team turned up. I had to hide in that copse for hours. I sat there all day with one bottle of water before I was eventually extracted and my team arrested them.'

Andy remained in the police until 2019, where he was hoping eventually to gain accreditation as a detective. However, once he was a detective constable in the Southend, Essex force, things took a serious turn for the worse with his career trajectory.

He was dismissed for selling special equipment.

'Google me. I was exonerated.'

It's a complicated story, but the indisputable outcome was that Andy needed to find a new job in the private sector.

'When I was first dismissed on 1 February 2019 I had a beer and a Chinese. I felt relaxed. Then I did my close protection course. I did really well, my military head kicked in. I got my SIA Close Protection Licence.'

To add to this, SSAFA, the Armed Forces charity, have been very supportive to him as a veteran. They bought him an £800 camera, so he has an AX53 Sony camera, which is vital for his work.

Having gained his SIA licence Andy swiftly got some celebrity clients, looking after VIPs including Professor

Green, James Morrison and Jools Holland. He accumulated knowledge fast, and varied and exciting assignments followed, during many of which he was not afraid to get his hands dirty. Sometimes literally.

He worked with Iraqis on a surveillance job to do with money laundering. Then in the next breath he was in Birmingham crawling down a driveway. He goes through bins. He got somebody back £90k in Bitcoin.

He put up his very first covert cameras: one in Birmingham and one in Kensington, and he has not stopped since: 'I retrieved a camera from a tree last weekend. I put it there to track an Asian guy living a double life with another family.'

For his ultra-high-net-worth clients, he does both close protection and counter surveillance. Respecting confidentiality is always key. 'All my work is based on recommendations. I am the go-to guy because I can do it all. If I need to put together a team, I try to use ex-Royal Marines, ex-police.'

As with Rik, surveillance bankrolled by suspicious spouses constitutes a lot of his bread and butter work.

'I do lots of matrimonial stuff. I've been following a rabbi. The rabbi's wife wanted a picture of the rabbi having sex at a hotel with a prostitute. The rabbi has a burner phone. I take money up front on those cases.'

This is because people get upset when they find out things they think they want to prove but in reality don't, and then do not wish to pay for such unwelcome information.

During their first meeting, Andy told Emma that he was on a live job with a barrister. He was using a 'ghost camera', and readily explained the advantages of this device for surveillance.

'A ghost camera is a little tiny camera. It can be built into a first-aid kit, a Wi-Fi speaker, a box folder. I have put devices in key fobs and coffee cups too. You can connect it to the Wi-Fi. Bug sweeps don't turn it up. They sweep cars for tracking devices but they won't find a ghost camera. I have spent over £1000 on kit for this barrister.'

Another nifty gadget is what in the police they call an IMSI-catcher, or 'IMSI-grabber' as Andy terms it. It is an international mobile subscriber identity-catcher, a telephone eavesdropping device that can be used for intercepting mobile phone traffic and tracking the location data of mobile phone users. They are also known as 'stingrays'. It is expensive but it is something else that can form a very useful part of your surveillance toolkit nowadays.

With the surveillance on the rabbi, the rabbi's security became suspicious and swept his car, but the devices were so discreet and high spec that they did not find either the tracking device or the listening device.

To maintain focus on these very different, often exhausting jobs, Andy tries to 'keep his eyes on the prize' and focus on his ultimate goal or objective at all times. Andy always says to himself: 'What objective do you need?'

Andy pointed out to Emma that there are two different

basic levels to surveillance. Level 2 surveillance is foot. Level 1 surveillance is driving too, and you can be fast-tracked on to that.

He then went on to familiarise Emma with some of the lingo of covert work. For example, 'lifestyling' is when you stick a tracking device on your target's car and follow them around. This way you build a picture of a person and really get to know about their life and behavioural patterns.

Andy used this lifestyling as part of his toolkit when he was hired to do surveillance on a prominent media figure. Andy was gathering information to be shared with the tycoon's ex-wife.

'He said that he was going to the Ritz every day! Oh to have his life… I only charged £200 for that work, and that was a multi-million pound divorce!'

During this same job there was a very stressful incident that he described. He had a tracking device on the media figure compromised when he was watching one of his residences.

'My tracker had gone down so I had to have "eyes on". I knew that the gate opened for thirty seconds. I had tailgated a bloke in. I got the tracker back. Then it was the concierge who challenged me. You *never* run from anywhere. You hold your nerve and walk. You always need a cover story.' They reviewed the CCTV though because the concierge told his employer he had seen someone who was looking for him. Andy got away though.

Andy had done what's known as a 'profile change' on this occasion, too. In other words, he had put glasses and a baseball cap on!

Amongst the secretive companies that Andy has worked for is Black Cube. Black Cube describes itself as 'a select group of veterans from the Israeli elite intelligence units that specialises in tailored solutions to complex business and litigation challenges'. One stand-out, very high-level job he was given through them involved a contender for prime minister of a European nation.

The existing leader wanted the contender followed. Andy did so, and his surveillance revealed that the contender met the old, ousted prime minister. This type of intelligence was gold dust for the leader. Sadly, the existing leader, who is very pro-Russian, beat the contender and got another term.

Andy has worked for another big Israeli firm too, ICC, which involved surveillance on the civil courthouse by St Paul's. He wanted to ascertain who his subject was with, but could not go into any more detail on that case. He had got a couple of tracker deployments coming up too.

On another fascinating brief, Andy was tracking a northern football manager's wife. He left listening devices, including one he left behind that is still live in the manager's house. He stuck one in the manager's Rolls-Royce too. The manager was having an affair and wanted to confirm his wife was too, with her personal trainer, before he took the decision to leave her for his mistress.

Amongst the gifts and specialisms that Andy brings to his surveillance work is the ability to stay awake for inhumanly long amounts of time. How long?

'I've stayed awake for thirty-four hours. I drink a lot of Red Bull. I can survive in the back of a vehicle on cold rations, and defecating and urinating in there on a job.' When Emma first spoke to him, he had spent three solid days on private sector surveillance, which is not unusual but which certainly requires serious stamina levels.

The Regulation of Investigatory Powers Act 2000 is commonly known, just as Andy repeatedly referred to it, as RIPA. It governs the use of covert surveillance by public bodies, including 'covert human intelligence sources' (that's undercover agents to you and me), bugs, video surveillance and interceptions of private communications such as email, WhatsApp and phone calls. Very significantly, surveillance in the private sector is not covered by RIPA.

'As the private sector is not regulated, you can do things like put trackers on cars.'

There is another key difference to the way that you work as well. In the police, to follow someone, you might get five cars, one motorbike and one van, a huge amount of support in other words. Conversely, in the private sector it might be just two people.

'You have to get the tracking device on. The private sector relies heavily on tech, especially bugging devices and cameras.'

The private sector uses black cabs a lot in London too. How?

'You feed the subject [the person being watched] into a black cab and they don't realise that the cab is all hooked up with surveillance.'

Andy shared one particularly disturbing case that he worked on. A South African guy was sexually abusing his children. Their billionaire grandfather paid Andy's team to get into the flat and do surveillance, to either prove his terrible suspicions or set his mind at rest. To gain access to the property, Andy needed a disguise and a cover story.

'I had a fluorescent jacket on and a bunch of rat traps, and a toolbox. Someone held the door open for me because I said, "There's a problem with rats around here because of the pandemic." People believe you. I wore a mask too.'

In this manner, you can be 'overt to be covert too: stick a fluorescent jacket on'. There were cameras in the rat traps. I had a recce on the covert camera. My team rented the next-door flat for six months. I broke into the subject's flat and put a camera and Wi-Fi into the house. I can pop locks under letterboxes.'

There was a little girl and a little boy and, sadly, Andy confirmed that their father was abusing them both. The girl was only four and the boy was younger. According to Andy, the client wanted him to play with the paedophile father's mind. Andy put fifteen different people into different scenarios to do so.

'The father wore a *Scream* mask when he abused the children. He liked ladyboys as well. So I set up a motorbike to go past with a *Scream* mask. A jogger with a *Scream* mask. Another time the father walked out of his flat and got into an Uber. I had set up two ladyboys. They held a *Scream* mask up and said "Leave those kids alone." The guy went mad.'

Emma caught up with Andy again a few months later, in June 2022, and his update on his adventures in surveillance did not disappoint. Since we last spoke, Andy had been arrested for kidnap.

He was working with a company that worked for Prince Naseem as a client. Naseem's car was broken into in Westbourne Grove. Credit cards, house keys and so on were taken from inside the vehicle. Andy wanted to know 'who the enemy was', so he used a tracking app on Naseem's stolen 3rd generation AirPods. This allowed him to track them to an address in Potters Bar.

At the address, number 67, Andy found an Albanian lady and her husband. Andy sensed immediately that they were not the people he was looking for. They were definitely not right. They told him that it was next door, who were 'shitbags', that he really wanted. Andy went with a couple of bodyguards and knocked on the neighbour's door. He had an Amazon box in his hand and a yellow jacket as a cover story.

Andy was talking to the guy who opened the door when

another guy suddenly came down the stairs with a gun. Andy grabbed and held the first guy in a neck hold, using him as a human shield. Both Andy's team and the people in the house called the police. Andy had also notified the police three hours prior to visiting the address, but despite this he was arrested and put into police custody. Andy ended up being charged with kidnap, false imprisonment and common assault.

'I did not intend to go and kidnap him. I stepped over the threshold, but that's trespass, not kidnapping.

"A black guy was with me. They cuffed him, but not me or a mixed-race guy who was also there. And that's it, they just grab the black guy and put cuffs on him, even though no one had been violent.'

The police took Andy's body camera and they have still not returned it.

'The police are snowflakes nowadays. They don't have any balls. The police are so slow too. It could be another two months before they look at my case. There are very strict rules in the SIA so for now I can't do CP.'

In other words, as a result of this incident, the police have taken his SIA licence away and he cannot do close protection. He has been driving NHS ambulances instead. He is also still doing private investigating.

In that latter role, he had been following a cash-in-transit van around because the client suspected that they were committing fraud.

'I spent four days on that watching the shop. The client was losing £200k daily and I was getting to know the characters. I did surveillance on a drunken lady too. I was trying to prove that she was an alcoholic in a custody battle where I was representing the father, and I found the evidence that I needed.'

Andy had been on another matrimonial case too. He stuck a camera up a lamppost, in that type of bold move that he characterises as overt to be covert. He put it up brazenly in the middle of the day, and got away with it by pretending that it was a traffic camera. This was to check on a guy who claimed that he was not living in the house but actually he was.

The psychology behind this type of thing, what he terms 'exposure meters' is interesting, in Andy's view.

'It's about fitting in with the environment.'

Andy cautions that this type of lower-level close protection work is fraught with risks and danger, though.

'A guy ran at me with a knife once. I took it off him, God knows how. It's not worth it for 12 to 13 quid an hour. Surveillance is £30 an hour.'

We appreciated Andy's openness about how precarious this type of existence could be. We also learned to take a closer look at lampposts and men claiming to be pest control!

## Chapter 14

# THE WEAPONS

Having learned all about surveillance gadgets, we had plenty more to learn from our contributors about weapons too.

The counter-terrorism police wear Kevlar body armour and carry the highest tech weapons available, including automatic assault rifles, sniper rifles, handguns, submachine guns and Tasers. Other top-of-the-range support gear they have access to includes battering rams and heavy-duty cutting equipment.

Private close protection officers, however, can't carry arms in the UK, and have to rely on their training and instincts instead. For an elite UK bodyguard like Josh, for example: 'Your best weapons are your brain and your eyes.'

Jonathan was in the middle of a heart-stopping covert MASTS (mobile armed support to surveillance team) while filming his TV show as he followed the trail of an individual believed to be armed.

He visited a counter-terror police training base. It is designed to instil military-style tactics into everyday police officers. Explosive entry used to be a tactic used only by the SAS. In the UK today, all armed police officers are trained in how to blow doors off with plastic explosives.

On the subject of weapons, according to Chris, 'comparisons between us and the American police are quite annoying. *Now* in the US they are meant to de-escalate. British police always try to de-escalate. We try to use pepper spray. I've never even tasered anyone, I've certainly never shot anyone. I've hit someone with my baton, I've punched people. The last thing you want to do is pull that trigger. You try to take a person down. The Taser…when people see the red dots on their chest they back down!

'People under the influence, who do strange things, they can be tasered by British officers. These officers can fire rubber bullets too.'

With rubber bullets in the UK, fired from a riot gun called a 'launcher', you aim at the belt buckle. But Chris has seen journalists at US protests with facial injuries from rubber bullets. So where are they firing them? The launcher has only been fired *twice* in all of Chris's time in the Northants police force.

He pointed out that police dogs can be weapons too. 'They're scary!' Chris has seen lots of police officers get bitten by dogs. When the dog handler says they are releasing the dogs, the police officers go silent. That's because if they are shouting, the dog thinks they are being aggressive and bites them.

Chris got tasered a little while ago. He was dealing with a violent chap, grappling on the floor, another police officer was handling a Taser and Chris got hit on the leg. It was quite a shock! A Taser needs to be within two inches of your skin to be effective.

'It's the classic red mist. I've seen it a couple of times. I've never had to step in having seen something horrific. You want to handcuff to the rear, if you handcuff to the front they can hit you! A fifteen-year-old did that to me once. They struck me in the face!'

We asked Valery if he thought more police should be armed in the UK? His response was typically clear and passionate. '*No* to arming more people but *yes* to pepper spray. That never killed anyone. Little things can save a life, but this is classified as a firearm! You can face two years in prison for carrying pepper spray.' He compared the situation with guns in the US. 'They are everywhere. You can have an M16 across your chest and buy an ice cream. In Vermont there is no licence required. The mentality here in the UK is a bit different. It's all about self-defence equipment, with kit like stun guns and pepper spray.'

In England and Wales, the guidance force by force on which specific weapons are used is provided by the Home

Office and ACPO, but ultimately the decision is made by the chief constable of any given force, which means different forces use a variety of different weapons. In Northern Ireland, the PSNI issues a Glock 17 pistol to all of its police officers. Interestingly, officers in Northern Ireland are also allowed to carry their issue sidearm off-duty.

When he has been in situations that permitted a firearm, Josh's choice was clear, too: 'I never used to fire automatic because it's not accurate. You only use it on the range.'

Simon Chesterman, the national lead on armed policing, told Jonathan during the filming of the Ross Kemp TV show that he believes if the threat level continues to increase, all officers could end up being armed. This is partly down to public and media pressure to act. He said if there are more armed police, it will inevitably lead to more police shooting incidents.

'Ultimately, they don't discharge firearms very often, these are not trigger-happy people. However, if you put more armed officers out there, inevitably we're going to get to more high-risk incidents quicker, and the chances are we will see more police shootings.'

Each of Jonathan's first trips to the armed police units around the country followed a similar pattern. He would be greeted by senior officers and communications people. They would drink tea and talk. Then he would be taken, usually by a massive, friendly and grizzled armed officer to the armoury to be shown their big weapons. The kit was incredible. Shiny racks of carbine rifles and ammunition at the force's disposal. The startling weight of a Glock pistol when you handle it. After that it would be a hanger or garage area to see their high-performance bulletproof vehicles. From there, they would return to an office to drink more tea and talk about the filming process.

No organised crime group gets close to this level of training, expertise and firepower. The ranges, the huge indoor training centre near Wakefield. There, inside a vast hanger, exists a life-size street and houses for police to practise sieges, armed entry and other scenarios. Or the Wales training centre, where Jonathan went for filming with elite counter-terrorist specialist firearms officers (CTSFOs), where they learn to blow the doors off with plastic explosives and are trained to the standards of the SAS.

This is truly an elite breed. Highly trained, military in demeanour, ruthless and focused. They need to be.

Counter-terrorist specialist firearms officers get deployed to the most dangerous national situations whether they be terrorist, drug or other major incident-related. These men – and even in the 2020s they usually are still men – can't give their names. They work with the intelligence services, the military and the police. These tough, highly trained good guys are out there looking after the public. They are prepared and equipped to do whatever is necessary to protect them.

A surprising aspect of the British armed police is

the regional variations and quirks. Whilst London and Birmingham have the kind of numbers, depth and dedicated expertise that might be expected, in other areas officers have to take on a much more varied role. In the countryside, the armed police are more likely to be called out because a depressed farmer has been sighted wandering into the wilds with a shotgun.

As all bodyguards know, it's a very different story in the US. As Brett put it: 'What can I have in the United States that I cannot have in other countries? Number one would be a weapon. Here in California and across the United States we have the ability to have a concealed weapon, a firearm. When we're in other countries we are not permitted to have one. Some countries don't even have firearms period. So that makes things somewhat difficult, but then that's when your verbal Judo comes in to talk to people as well.'

The perfect bodyguard is a chameleon, who can adapt to their new surroundings fast. The rules around weapons change as you travel from place to place. It can be controversial on your home turf too.

As a bodyguard, Brett is allowed to carry a weapon in LA 'and that's a very touchy subject as well. Especially in the city of Los Angeles, if you cannot get a concealed weapon or gun permit, you have to meet some very strict criteria. I know police officers who left the job early and let their stuff expire. They have a hard time getting it back. So if Joe Citizen comes and tries, especially from another country, to get a concealed weapon… It's not going to happen. Not in the city of LA. He or she may get it through the county, which is a little bit easier, depending on who the sheriff is at the time. But it's very difficult in New York. You can't get one in several places within Washington, DC, either.

'There are several places within the United States that you cannot get one now, that take it a step further. Like, I have a Utah concealed weapon permit, as well as in Arizona. I was covered in every state with the exception of California, New York and Washington [DC] on the licence. Now I'm covered here in California as well. And I have people in New York and I have people in Washington, so I don't have to worry about it, but it is just that those three places, you cannot.'

When Brett comes to the UK, no bodyguards are allowed weapons. It doesn't matter whether you're looking after a Russian billionaire, a Saudi Arabian prince or an A-list Hollywood actor, you've got to leave the firearm at home.

'You have to leave them at home. Yes, absolutely. To be honest with you [in] all my years of bodyguarding, I think I've come across two or three altercations, where I actually needed a gun. And I've travelled all over the world. You have just got to learn how to talk to people. And you just have to have a demeanour. You can't go around pushing some people because people don't like to be touched. And if you do that, you escalate the situation versus if I just sit down and we talk. We have a short conversation, you get more respect that way. And I did that as a police officer also. I try to talk to people, but certain people you just can't talk to, let's face it.'

As Britain's new monarch King Charles III greeted fans outside Buckingham Palace on Friday, 9 September 2022, a certain member of his security team caught the attention of TikTok users. In a video that gathered 6.4 million views within days, the bodyguard steps out of the monarch's car and reveals a golden gun secured on his belt. With his perfectly groomed silver beard and steely stare, he's hard to miss. Part of the 'ring of steel' protecting the new king, he never strays more than a metre from the monarch's side but his personal identity remains shrouded in mystery.

The weapon that attracted so much attention on TikTok was the 9 mm Glock 17 pistol that is carried by all armed personal protection officers (PPOs), a role within the Royalty Protection Group. This squad from Scotland Yard are provided by the Metropolitan Police and are specially trained to protect the royal family both at home and abroad.

Unlike the distinctive red jacket and helmet worn by the Honourable Corps of Gentlemen at Arms, PPOs are much less noticeable in their plainclothes uniform. Their training is also vastly different and includes unarmed combat, emergency first aid and advanced driving. Besides their Glock 17 pistols, the team of PPOs are also required to carry a radio and first-aid kit with them at all times. The PPOs select their own code names for their royal clients and are always seen working together effectively, walking in formation as they move royals through crowds and to new locations.

Integral to the role of a PPO is a close relationship with the principal, the royal they are tasked with protecting. Although it is unclear how long this mysterious bodyguard has been working under King Charles III, he has been spotted by the royal's side for many years. Always maintaining his cool demeanour, the strong rapport between the two enables them to communicate non-verbally. In order to detect an emergency within seconds, he must be able to read King Charles's body language and the body language of people in a crowd. The bodyguard and his team extensively and meticulously plan every single event Charles attends. This involves completing a recce of the venue, memorising the arrivals and departures, and locating the nearest hospital as well as the three most effective routes to it. As Charles begins his reign as King, the stakes will be even higher for this enigmatic bodyguard, as he is now protecting one of the most high-profile people in the world.

## Chapter 15

# PROTECTING THE ROYALS

In addition to the aforementioned unexpected TikTok star, and the operation with Prince Harry that opened the book, there are many other notorious examples of the curious relationship between royals and close protection. Did Diana have an affair with one of her bodyguards? How does it feel to be a bodyguard to the Sultan of Brunei's son when he's invited Michael Jackson to his birthday party?

Look closely at any picture of a member of the royal family in public duty. You will spot the personal protection officers who must guard them at risky public appearances. For a member of the British royal family, potentially that means *any* public appearance.

All royal protection officers, those assigned to members of the government, former prime ministers, ambassadors, visiting heads of state, and other individuals deemed to be at risk are serving members of the Met, with at least ten to fifteen years of experience before entering this highly specialised field.

The royal family are protected throughout their entire life, in public and private, every day of the year. They even have a protection officer assigned to them at home. The Protection Command is one of the commands within the Specialist Operations directorate of London's Metropolitan Police Service. Essentially for our story, and in contrast to the vast majority of UK police officers, all members of the Protection Command are authorised firearms officers (AFOs), and many of them routinely carry firearms in the course of their duties. Its specialism is protective security and there are two branches.

These two distinct branches were formed by merger as recently as April 2015, to provide a more effective service. The first branch, as explained earlier, is Royalty and Specialist Protection, or RaSP, which provides protection to the royal family as well as close protection to government officials. These officials can really be any political VIPs considered to be at risk, so the Prime Minister, obviously, but also government ministers, ambassadors and visiting heads of state. RaSP officers are to be found providing armed security at the royal residences too. They serve in London but also Windsor Castle, Balmoral and other Scottish royal homes. Furthermore, RaSP operates the Special Escort Group.

The second branch is Parliamentary and Diplomatic

Protection, or PaDP, which provides uniformed security to government buildings, officials and diplomats. PaDP provides both armed and unarmed protection of the Parliamentary Estate, embassies and missions, as well as residential protection for government ministers if it is considered to be required. PaDP are the branch who control, for example, who can get in and out of Downing Street and New Scotland Yard. Police Constable Keith Palmer, who died in the 2017 terrorist attack on Westminster, was a member of the PaDP Command.

Chris has done close protection of royals and VIPs and if there is one thing you learn, he says: 'In CP you *plan the life* out of everything. There is no space for surprises or the unexpected, you need complete control. You have weeks to plan a visit, and to mitigate all the risk as much as you can. To use the swan analogy, you are calm on the surface, but the legs are frantically paddling underneath. Say you have four venues, and you plan an hour at each venue. You recce the venues and you recce the routes. When you land at the venue, you have your meet-and-greet. Politicians don't mind an early finish. Sometimes it overruns: then you have to plan the next bit of it. It's really interesting work.'

Royals and political VIPs are notoriously vulnerable on walkabouts, which most CP officers dread. With royals encouraging the public to approach them, everyone is on high alert. Arriving at and leaving venues are also notorious points of vulnerability. At any sign of danger, the royal protection officer must move at lightning speed to either shelter them back in their vehicle or race for cover in the building that they are entering. The schedules of royals and politicians are often to some degree public knowledge, so royal protection have to be one step or more ahead of individuals who may have familiarised themselves with itineraries and mean harm.

Like any close protection work, royal protection involves exceptionally careful planning, and, of course, contingency planning for any dangerous curveball that you have to assume may arise. You have to be prepared for vehicle breakdown, traffic, roadworks, flying bullets or a bomb going off. Where is the nearest hospital? Part of securing the area is watching the public for suspicious activity. Why would someone be wearing a thick jacket on a warm day, what are they concealing? What are people doing with their hands, what are they watching?

Royal protection officers are assigned to a member of the family. Some officers have long term assignments with a particular royal, while others move between them on a roster basis. British royal family work is varied, tiring and involves a great deal of planes, trains and automobiles. It is not uncommon to have the royals divide their time between London, the south-east and Scotland in the course of a week, or even a day, and the quality of protection, recces and communication has to be consistent. And bulletproof.

Officers learn to look out for threats from unexpected

sources as well as the obvious ones. When Prince Harry was at Silverstone, Chris tells us: 'The place where the principal was having photos taken was right under the press gang walk. I wasn't worried about him being shot, I was worried about a camera falling on his head!'

At the London 2012 Olympics, Chris was a close protection officer for a few months. Big events like that are different from something like policing a royal walkabout. They are more about large-scale screening and control. He was looking after a very high-ranking visiting dignitary.

'They wanted to do something that was not *illegal* but that would have pushed the boundaries: if they get away with that, other countries will want to do it. We had to prevent it. Sarah was pregnant with our third child, pregnant and uncomfortable.'

Sarah happily takes over this story, which has entered their family lore.

'There was a really famous phone call that I have never let Chris forget. He phones me from the Olympics and it was the Super Saturday day and he was looking after Kate and Wills as a close protection officer and he has had the best day. It's hot. I am pregnant and I am making dinner with two children hanging off me. Chris is like, "I met Kate today" and he pauses and then says, "She is just so attractive." "Is she Chris?" I said. "Is she?" But he goes on like I hadn't understood. He was like, "No you don't understand, I don't mean just a bit attractive I mean up close she is just so slim and so attractive." He didn't get it. But he did send me flowers afterwards.'

Chris smiles. 'Sarah won't let me forget that one!'

Despite these amusing wrong notes, the 2012 Olympics was great for Chris. 'I'm a close protection officer, and this was a fascinating, really interesting job! There was loads of work going on behind the scenes to make everything okay. We were protecting one high ranking member of the royal family and a drunk guy tried to get in the car. We did *everything* to mitigate risk. The Olympics was great. People didn't realise that the armoury was underneath the flower market! In the morning, we would take the guns out and get armed up. I knew the guy planning the visit.'

Chris ended up in the royal box at the stadium. On Super Saturday he saw Jessica Ennis and Mo Farah win their races. Arnold Schwarzenegger came in too and, Chris says, 'He was a really nice bloke.'

Sometimes when you are guarding the royals, British or overseas visitors, you try and find a cover story as a close protection officer, to be less conspicuous. At the London 2012 Olympics Chris was assigned to a female member of a foreign royal family. She made him go around Harrods with her while she looked at swimwear.

'We spent hours looking at ladies' clothing and perfume. It was awkward. Someone asked me where the haberdashery section was! We like to work going under the radar with no one noticing what we are doing. If I'm protecting somebody, ideally you want that bubble. But if the principal's image is to go and interact with people…'

These royal shopping trips can go wrong. Ejeneca told us that she knew people who have lost their clients in Selfridges and Harrods! One spent a very anxious twenty minutes looking for her. Ejeneca had also heard many stories from colleagues about royal clients from Bahrain and the UAE buying dogs while in the UK. 'The nanny ends up looking after the dog. It's another factor when you are out and about too.'

Chris knows the specific division of the Met that is just close protection very well. He's had plenty of professional interface with them on royal, diplomatic and ministerial protection. The work always involves loads of recces of the venues. You have to know the venues inside out.

If Chris and Sarah's force in Northamptonshire receives a VIP, then the Met, or other dedicated force, depending on who the principal is, travel to the county. Personal protection is provided by the Met and the Northamptonshire force provides the protective ring around it. Ex-prime ministers always have protection, and they get royal visits in Northamptonshire too.

Chris told us what so many of our other contributors said, and in this case it's not like TV and the movies. 'You are *desperate* for nothing to happen on close protection. Normally you *want* something cool to happen. On one royal visit a dog slipped through Prince William's legs and we had to catch it.'

Then there was one incident in which Chris, as the close protection, had to intercept a suspicious character who tried to get in a principal's car.

'These are high-powered people driven by meticulous schedules. I know officers who have been probed by members of the royal family about the direction being taken.' The officers have to reassure them that it is all for necessary safety reasons.

'If you're hosting a royal event in the country, you might have one protected person, but they bring their kids and their friends. It's good to have rapport with your principal.' One of Chris's very first visits was with Princess Anne at an equestrian event.

'Her PPO said he was going off to the toilet and he disappeared for twenty minutes. Suddenly I was her CP officer. The stress levels went through the roof! Sometimes people are just being awkward or difficult.'

Most royals understand the pressures, however, and that their lives are in capable hands. On another occasion Chris was driving a quite high-ranking royal family member. She sat in the back. She was adamant that she did not want to run a red light.

As Chris points out, with the royals, you have to remember that 'it's about protecting *image* as well as safety. In the same way, you can't park in a disabled bay. The pressure on people driving principals is *massive*. You don't want them having control of their electric windows.

We are *lucky* in the UK that the threat level against these people is low.'

Royal protection officers are highly trained in defensive driving. In fact, there are a number of different courses: basic driver, response driver, advanced driver, anti-hijack driver and armoured car driver. You can learn loads of techniques to get out of hazards. Convoy driving. Putting a protection bubble around the cars. For Chris's training they hired an airfield and had the trainee officers driving slalom through cones. They use cars for training that are about to get scrapped, because the vehicles tend to get pretty bashed up.

Getting into royal protection involves some serious vetting and training. Six months of initial training, not to mention specialist further training courses, maybe thirty further weeks over your career, covering firearms handling, unarmed combat, contingency planning, situational awareness and emergency first aid. The weapon of choice is often a side-holstered Glock 17, carried discreetly.

US bodyguard Brett has had his fair share of interactions with royals too.

'Well, my typical week pre-Covid was pretty hectic.'

Brett was busy all the time, not with just one particular client; he might have a couple of clients doing something on different days that wanted him and he had to schedule around. He was keen to get back to the usual hectic existence for his company that constituted his 'normal'.

'We were pretty busy and I hope for that to pick up again,

to be busy 24/7, flying around the globe or just bodyguarding somebody... Having the dignitaries come back to LA once Covid is lifted, Saudis and people from Abu Dhabi or whatever the case may be. Princes, kings, queens. Coming back to Los Angeles and started giving us a call again.'

## Chapter 16

# BRETT

> **'He terrified my client. I had to put her in the room
> and go down and sit with this guy and persuade him to
> go back to Germany and never be seen again. Sometimes
> you have to threaten people to get your word across.'**

This intriguing character who we have codenamed Brett, got into the business many years ago after being a police officer for the Los Angeles Police Department (LAPD). He was there for many years, but prior to his retirement, he did personal protection for other companies and individuals. Eventually he opened up his own security and personal protection company. This background means he can see both the differences and similarities between the LAPD work and personal protection, as well as their shared objectives.

'We both have the same goal in this. That's just to protect

the citizens and for me it's more of a one-on-one to protect my clients and their families. I take it a step further too. You wear so many hats, especially if you are with the same person for years. You find yourself in the role of a manager when the manager can't travel, or you find yourself as the publicist when the publicist can't travel. I find myself more of an asset protector than just a normal bodyguard. You just have to run the whole gamut. You can't have tunnel vision, because there's other things you have to get involved with, without being too overprotective. You have to think outside the box a lot. And that's what I like to do. I like to gain the trust of my clients, I think outside the box for their safety, their family's safety and their assets as well.'

We asked Brett how he built his team up to what it is today.

'I'm still building the team. I don't just take anybody off the street and say, "Hey, stand here and be a bodyguard." That's not the type of company I run. I don't want to put my clients in that type of position, or to get sued. My personnel, my staff, my employees are 100 per cent legit. If I say they're from retired or active LAPD, they are. I don't just say that because I'm retired LAPD. Do I give the illusion that everybody else on my staff is? Like some of these other companies out there? No. My guys and my girls are *known*.'

Thorough background checks are carried out, Brett explained, in case they aren't from LAPD and they come from another department or from somewhere else around the world. 'Just like other big companies, including the FBI: fingerprints, knowledge of people, references. They go through sexual-harassment training, first aid, shooting skills, common knowledge skills, and self-defence skills. Especially with the new company that I'm starting, we train everybody the same way. We don't want anybody saying they weren't trained and we don't want any clients out there in limbo or in jeopardy. Non-disclosure is a piece of paper. Knock on wood and hope we never have to do that, but if we have to, we will put you in jail, and we'll be 100 per cent behind the client on everything. If you did something that was wrong to jeopardise the client or the contract…'

In Los Angeles, Brett's core team consists of one female and two other males. That's not his whole team – he 'has a slew of people now'– but they are his inner circle. With the female such a vital component of the team, we wanted to hear from Brett about gender preferences on jobs, too.

'It's non-gender, but most people feel more comfortable with men than women. But you know, let's face it, we go to a nightclub somewhere and my client needs to go to the restroom and the restroom is very crowded. I can't go in there with her, you know, so I got a female with me. They can go into the restroom with a female client during the standby, making sure nobody takes pictures or harasses them in the bathroom.'

Does the gender of the bodyguard play a part in what private clients want? It was a question we were keen to put to

Brett, since his business had worked with huge female stars. Do his most senior female co-workers or the female bodyguards in his team get treated differently by people in the business?

Brett didn't hesitate.

'My females get treated the same way. I don't know how they are looked at by the client. I know I get some clients who love a female and are happy to see a female, and some clients just want to have somebody who can fight, whatever the case may be. However, this is not always the best client to have anyway.'

To this point, Brett reminded us that bodyguards sometimes vet their clients just as much as clients vet their bodyguards.

'I don't do rappers because I don't want to get in a fight or a shooting every time I step into a venue. So that's a policy that my company has. We don't want to fight, to have the fighter pull out guns, or stuff like that. We just want to pick and choose whoever is representing this company, have them represent the company, and the client is happy with that. Whether it's male or female, this is what we're putting out there.'

We wanted to learn more about whether different clients had different priorities. What's the variation between what everyone is really worried about?

For Brett, 'At the end of the day, clients hire us for safety, to make it from point A to point B and then back home to point A again. Safe and sound with no problems. It could be your A-list celebrity worrying about paparazzi and stalkers, or just anxious about being seen, which goes with the nature of the beast. Or it could be your quiet CEO, who's a multimillionaire and runs a hedge-fund company. They hire us to do the same thing: it's to provide safety.

'Sometimes we are called in for staff meetings at different companies where they are going to terminate employment of an individual and they want us standing by just in case that individual decides to go off on them or be very hostile. They have security right there to take care of the business at that particular point. We do security for different companies. Apple may call and say, "We need somebody to escort the trucks or the Apple product that's just coming out." We may pick that up from the airport, and follow the trucks to different venues.'

Brett has long-term relationships with many of these clients, generated by his expertise and professionalism.

'I'm still continuing with many of the different clients. I used to do the Victoria's Secret million-dollar bra once a year for the fashion show. They would actually take that bra on tour with one of the Victoria's Secret models, but I was the one that was handling the bra and the briefcase hands-on. We've been all over the United States on different television shows with the bra and stuff like that. So it's just different things. But at the end of the day, it's all about safety, the safety of the individual or the safety of their product.

And we make sure that we return home safe and sound with whatever the case may be.'

Is this how Brett has built the kind of loyalty he has with the A-list socialites he's looked after?

'Well, you build your reputation and rapport with the client with trust. They have to be able to trust you as a bodyguard, not only with their lives, but with their assets. They want to be able to go out, have fun, party, whatever the case could be, especially females. And you have to be that person who is not going to take advantage of them. If they are intoxicated, you're not going to try to take pictures of them. You're not going to try to extort them for money. I mean, this is a trust relationship that has to be built and your reputation has to be built.'

Building a relationship can take time. 'No one's going to trust you right off the bat, but once you are around them for a while, then they feel you out just like you feel them out. Then the trust factor definitely comes into play. And that's a great thing because if you can't trust your client or your client can't trust you, then it could be a long, miserable day for everybody.'

Brett knows what his clients want and what they don't want. With the potential to become a celebrity in his own right, with a TV show in the works, he has to tread carefully. 'If I'm with a client that would be a no-go, you couldn't do that because of their personal space. And they don't hire me to be in front of a camera for them. Personal/professional is a thin line with clients. You try to keep it professional but I'll be honest with you, if you're going to be a professional, then you have to get very close to your individual. Some call me "the big brother", some call me "dad".

'Their family members, manager, lawyer, publicist are always calling me to check something out, so you gotta have a real close relationship with all of them. I'm the go-to guy, so to speak. And especially since you have to do so many different things, they have to let me know what's going on so I can send my team out there to advance that situation.'

There are limits though. 'I won't go out to your party with you as a guest, but I will go out to your party as your body. God, you know what I mean? Don't put me on your guest list because that's not what I'm about. I'd rather stay home with my family, but if you need me to be your body, yeah, that's why I come in. Anything else is flattering, but no.'

Brett is pleased to say that, perhaps because of this delicate balancing act, he hasn't really experienced his celebrity private clients crossing boundaries. There were points where he can see how it would have happened though.

'One of my clients, of course while I was working, invited my wife and my kids to Disneyland and we had season passes already, but we had the best experience with her. We had red carpet treatment everywhere. We went on numerous rides by the back door. So that was really nice.'

Brett's clients come from all over the place these days. 'I have A-list celebrities here in LA, but I also have CEOs, some around the world. I have dignitaries from Dubai, Abu Dhabi, Saudi, we get families coming in quite a bit. I also have assets out there as well to do security when I can't make it.'

We wondered if it was different work being a bodyguard for a celebrity as opposed to, say, a CEO. Does the role that Brett or his team play differ with the different types of people that they're protecting? He assured us that some things are constant, whoever the client.

'The bottom line is protection, but the roles do change. Sometimes we have to drive, but sometimes we hire one of my professional drivers as well as a bodyguard. It just depends on the client. They may want different things, A-list clients especially can want different things. Most of them want to be photographed by paparazzi. That's a different world. The more quiet ones, you don't really know who they are, unless it's Elon Musk. For the most part you're bodyguarding them as personal protection because anything can happen at any given time, but nobody really wants bodyguards until they really need them. By that time it could be too late.'

Celebrities are more worried about stalkers. 'There can be people overwhelming them, taking advantage of them, jumping on them, and robbing them. I'm worried that they carry a lot of money with them. Maybe they have documents with them that need protecting. Maybe they go into a meeting that could turn hostile. So they just need to be protected because they have that type of clout. At the end of the day, they hire us to be their protector.'

Much like what many in the UK see as a dilution of quality in close protection after the Olympics, Brett has his doubts about quality control in the USA too.

'I don't want to be anywhere where there's a bunch of Americans because, let's face it, there's a security company opening up here in California every other week, from bouncers to police to just somebody who wants to do security. I don't stay as competitive because the real professional guys, you can tell us apart, of course. You get some of these guys who undercut the budget and then the celebrity ends up paying for it.

'You take a situation where Kim Kardashian was in Paris and her place got robbed and they tied her up or whatever the case may be, we take that kind of stuff very seriously. We don't want to leave a client alone, even if this client says, "Hey, go pick up such and such from the venue and I'll be okay here." That does not fly. If I'm here to protect you, I'm here to protect you. And that's the way it has to be. It needs extra security. We have to bring in extra for family members, which I have done quite often. Especially when I was in Dubai, when they had the whole family there, I had to call in some reinforcements to come and take care of the rest of the family the same way I took care of my client.'

A life like Brett's brings glamour but danger too. Did his family only see the upsides of his work, being wholly supportive of his fascinating job, or did they have their doubts?

'Let's say they enjoy what I do because they get an opportunity to meet celebrities and different people that they probably wouldn't normally get to meet. They get to be the envy of their friends. Depending on the situation, their friends can even tag along and meet the celebrities as well. My kids have talked to me about possibly being bodyguards in the future.

'One thing I want to see them do is go to school, get that education first, and don't follow in my footsteps – be better than my footsteps! Get that business degree, take over this company and take it to the next level. By meeting people and doing the right things, with education. My daughter is very headstrong. She works with me every once in a while. When I have a client who's having a big party, she may go and do the guest list for me at the front door. She's pretty bad ass already. Probably a chip off the old block sometimes, that cracks me up.'

Brett's long LAPD career paid off. 'It's funny because I often run across A-list celebrities. They hire foreign military personnel. That's good if I was in Israel, but when you come to LA, you have to know the streets exactly. You can punch up the address on your phone and it gets you there, but what Waze does not tell you is the danger that's on that street. How many gangs are there in that particular direction you're taking? If you're going to save time

and go through downtown LA, how many gang neighbourhoods do you have to pass? Gang-infested neighbourhoods
in Inglewood and the surrounding areas, with the Bloods
and the Crips. You really have to know the lay of the land.
Even when I go abroad, I make sure I hire locals to show
me around. Am I going to London? I hire my local guy to
be with me.'

We wanted to know what feels different about close
protection in the USA, Asia, Eastern Europe, South America.
We learned that being a bodyguard in the Middle East is
different to anywhere else. The fundamental responsibility
to protect and serve might be the same, but we were
astonished, and sometimes unnerved, to learn about what
close protection looks like in other places. It gave us an even
greater respect for the exceptional discipline, training and
conduct of British close protection officers, widely believed
to be the best in the world.

Brett had plenty to say to us about his experiences in
South America and the Middle East.

'Oh my God. Mexico City. I've been there for work too
many times. Mexico City is a rough place, but if you surround
yourself with the right people, then you have no worries. I've
been to Beirut bodyguarding, even on the 4th of July with
[my A-list celebrity] and I was like, "oh my God, this is not
happening." But, you know, we pulled it off. I didn't want
to go. Her family didn't want us to go. But at the end of the
day, it's her choice, you know? So, once again, we had good

people from there who helped us out tremendously. So it turned out to be a good trip but those are the places I never thought I would be bodyguarding, especially in Lebanon at night. No way. Especially one of my buddies, he's from Tel Aviv and I'll try to get him to go and he says, "Are you crazy? They'll cut my head off at the airport." And I'm like, "Oh, I didn't know." Some things you just don't realise, but, wow. I'm living here under my bubble. It's very interesting.'

Brett would agree with Ejeneca about the importance of teamwork and collaboration too, especially when preparing for a major event. 'For big events, I don't do any special security. Everything is pretty much a carbon-copied blueprint because we want to make sure we don't skip anything. We've got a checklist but if you go into a red carpet event we like to have an advance team there. Normally I have somebody that I know who has worked for me in the past or still works for me or is maybe working for the venue. Normally we have somebody already on the red carpet that we can turn to and get some direction from. We know them very well. We're tailoring events to the venue.'

It's about thinking ahead, being prepared. 'If we can, especially if we're out of the country, we always advance and see what's the best way in and the best way out in case of emergency. We scour the neighbourhood looking for escape routes and making sure we don't go into any cul-de-sacs. We try to get the local police department or the local big security company to give us a hand if we are out of state somewhere. That's pretty much it, we just want to make sure that everybody's safe.

'We try to get their itinerary, an agenda for our clients every day. "Hey, what's going on today?" If there's something on that agenda that we need to advance or something that doesn't look right, then we go and we scout it out. We may try to take a different route or if it was something really, really sketchy then we have to sit down and talk to management about it and say, "Hey, this is what's happening in this particular neighbourhood or close to this particular neighbourhood. Can we reschedule this today?" Or we may need to organise additional security for a particular location. And that's pretty much it.'

Brett has been on some very hazardous jobs, where he was personally responsible for averting harm coming to his asset. One of the most notable of them happened when he was overseas.

'I was surrounded by what we thought were all dignitary-type people. And some of them were, but some of the people overseas pretend to be royalty from different countries. And they flash a lot of money, but sometimes these people aren't who they say they are. You have no way of knowing at the time.

'One specific group tried to kidnap my client one night at a club. And that was a very, very scary situation. I had to rely on some other bodyguards that were in the area. I had to rely on some management, too, to come in and try to intervene. That's all while I get my client and make an escape. They basically ran a diversion tactic for me inside of this nightclub and my client and I actually had to escape out of a different route. That situation could have been very, very hairy, very scary if I didn't think fast and reach out to other people that I knew from America to help me because it was just me by myself. It could've gotten a lot worse if they actually managed to kidnap my client that night.'

Whilst some jobs, like HS2, continued during the pandemic, the nightclub partying, celebrity walkabouts, and jaunts with fake foreign princes came to an abrupt halt. Of course it is not just the British police and bodyguards who get into these hairy situations. Brett has found himself in hot water on a number of different occasions worldwide.

'Yes. I've had some very difficult situations. In the past I've managed to escape different countries and I've escaped different problems where I've had to rely on instinct. I've had to rely on my undercover skills. I've had to rely on other bodyguards that just happened to be in the area at the time. Nothing is always easy! Certain things you do in this line of work can cause tension and people will always try to do some type of harm to your clients. So that's something that you have to be very aware of and you have to be able to react accordingly under any circumstances – you cannot lose your temper or lose your cool.'

Keeping a cool head in this kind of situation would be far beyond the capacity of most normal, untrained people, but for Brett and the safety of his clients, it is mission critical. On another occasion, a German stalker had travelled from Denmark to California to threaten Brett's client.

'He terrified my client. I had to put her in the room and go down and sit with this guy and persuade him to go back to Denmark, if he's travelled from there? and never be seen again. You know, you just have to talk to people. Sometimes you have to threaten people to get your word across. I wasn't harmed but I did have people around me that could make his life a little more miserable by putting him in jail or whatever the case may be, until we got out. So it's just certain situations that you have to deal with.'

When faced with a stalker or kidnap attempt, you would want someone as calm and collected as Brett protecting you.

## Chapter 17

# JOHN

**'Yes, you are going to be on a private jet in Sardinia, but you are going to miss your kid's first birthday. You have made that decision. Our industry is fast personal deployments. It's the job.'**

Like Brett, John Morrison is a figure with international stature in close protection, as well as physical stature. John is tall, dark-haired, imposing, and looks every inch his six-foot-four frame. He is a supremely confident speaker with a strong Glaswegian accent. He has a mischievous, almost Jack-the-lad air about him. He looks like he would be fun on a night out but also more than capable of protecting you if necessary.

He describes himself as a 'global family security consultant and advisor'. We asked him what this means. Essentially, he is a family security expert who specialises in global travel and security operations for private clients: high-net-worth families.

John has worked and consulted for some of the world's most wealthy and powerful families, which has not only allowed him to travel the world but also to advise on the entire spectrum of the security landscape. Specialising in family security, safety and welfare has seen him project managing on areas such as superyacht and private jet coordination and facilitation, staff training, recruitment and background checks, and implementation of family security services including security drivers, guards and close protection officers.

John's experience and international contacts started during his twelve years within the Royal Military Police, and then later grew organically during his time within the private security sector. He is a director and founder of the international security company Excellentia Global but has opted to continue operations rather than retire from physical deployments.

He is a highly motivated, skilled and professional close protection operative with a proven civilian and military operational, training and investigative background. Twelve years in the military police has led to an exceptional level of self-discipline, adaptability and the capacity to work in high-pressure and arduous situations, both nationally and internationally, in highly hostile countries.

During John's long service in the military police

he specialised in the art of infiltration into illegal and subversive organisations via undercover deployments. He was undercover infiltrating drug communities within the army itself too. Drugs are a big issue in the British Army and he was trained by SO10, an elite Met Police unit, to infiltrate drug gangs in the army and to bring them down from within. SO10 was the former designation of the Metropolitan Police's covert operations group.

As his career developed, he further progressed in the world of undercover operations by becoming a surveillance officer and, ultimately, a bodyguard for UK British Ambassadors. Whilst in the military he gained the rank of sergeant. He was deployed to Bosnia, Croatia, Kosovo, Iraq, Kenya and Sudan. Amongst other things, whilst in Iraq he was involved in the interviewing of known AQ terrorists and Iraqi insurgents.

John's career in the private sector has included deployments to places including Pakistan, Libya, the US, Russia, France, Belgium and the Cayman Islands. In 2016, he was the country security consultant for Hyundai during the European Championships in France, the 2018 World Cup in Russia, and more recently, the 2020 European Championships in London.

John Morrison wears numerous hats. One of them is that he organises and runs the Security and Networking conference for the close protection community and, on an overcast Saturday morning in November 2021, We went along to see what it was all about.

It was at the Victory Services Club in Seymour Street, central London, with a demographic which must have been at least 90 per cent extremely tall men. The delegates were all in smart dark suits or sports jackets and chinos. As we filed into the venue, he overheard snippets of chat: 'I looked after a Saudi family then a Kuwaiti family', 'two tours of Iraq', 'I've diversified into drone defence'…

Inside, a spiral staircase led down to a trade fair, with a table laid out with tactical gear, including military pens with special technology to break a window with the tip, pen knives and tactical vests. A treasure trove of reconnaissance devices featured the highlight of a suitcase that opened up to reveal a mobile surveillance control centre with three screens. Q would be jealous of some of this kit!

The stands in the hall included upmarket looking chauffeur services, a live firing weapons course, private jets, and CCTV systems hidden in metal suitcases. John Morrison explained that the event has been going for twelve years and is growing every year. More and more delegates arrived and the hall buzzed with chatter and engagement in this compelling, secret community.

We talked to Christopher Williams-Martin, the CEO of FlyEliteJets, a private jet company. Well spoken and wearing a smart blue double-breasted pinstripe tailored suit, Christopher's personal passion is helicopters and he is a hugely experienced pilot. Since Covid they had been even busier.

'Clients no longer want to show up at international airports and queue, they just want to turn up and go.'

Christopher also buys and sells private jets to clients and arranges close protection. Amongst his clients are Middle Eastern royalty and corporate CEOs – Nice, Malé, Doha and Dubai are some of his most popular routes. He owns midsize and super-midsize jets, and even ultra-long-range Gulfstreams that can fly anywhere in the world. The crown jewel of his fleet is the Boeing Business Jet. It has two bedrooms on board, showers, lounges and offices. It is ultra-luxurious billionaire travel. He describes it as 'out of this world'.

After this intriguing encounter with Christopher, we spoke to Matt Hellyer, the CEO of Frontier Risk Management. Matt was in his forties, with a northern accent, goatee beard and a firm handshake. As he explained: 'Risk covers all of the tradecraft. It has never felt more important.'

Matt has had police, military, NGOs, and even the head of security for Amazon coming on his courses. Of these, his most popular is the kidnap and ransom day, where one of you plays the negotiator and another the hostage: 'What happens if one of your clients gets kidnapped? These are important skills to learn.'

With a £3k price tag, you get a physical twelve-day course in groups, ending with writing a 5000-word dissertation. Not cheap but it sounds worth it. Matt was a paratrooper who passed selection to the SAS and then spent fifteen years in the regiment. He talked about what he does now: evacuation planning, crime scene management, crisis simulations, anything with a risk attached. He sees himself as creating the next generation of risk management professionals.

Next up was Paul Hughes, who runs Special Projects at Drone Defence Limited. With auburn hair, blue jeans and a checked shirt with a padded vest jacket, he was full of energy, a huge character who describes himself as a 'token Welsh ginger'. Formerly of the RAF and an ex-spy too, Paul speaks five languages and was in the same room as Saddam Hussein when he was a weapons inspector.

Now he works with drones. He looks at protecting national infrastructure sites and works with high-net-worth individuals on their drone defence capabilities. In his hand he held a small black box. It can take out any semi-autonomous drone. 'If someone is coming for you with a loaded drone then what are you meant to do? You have to take defensive measures.'

He passed him an expensive black box with a handle on the back, explaining that it was extraordinary what it was capable of. We asked Paul how much it cost.

'It retails at £12k,' he replied. 'Threat level 1 is the hobbyist drone operator, a member of the public or a paparazzi who, for example, is trying to take photos of a principal with a drone. Threats go up to level 4, which is major terrorism and state-sponsored drone attacks.'

He can take down any of their drones as well as intercept

and detect the command-and-control systems. Attack drones can now fly ninety miles an hour. The black box Jonathan was holding could be used to make the attack drone fall out of the sky.

'Imagine you're in a superyacht and the drone is on its way to your principal, it's basically an aerial Molotov cocktail. You hold up the defence shield box and you can either jam it so it loses comms and automatically returns to its taking-off point, or it's possible to jam and force a landing.'

Sky fences now exist around some prisons as they provide an effective force field around a site and jam the signal of any approaching drone. Paul laughed at that, explaining that in one prison near Dublin some of the wealthier prisoners were getting Deliveroo takeaways to their windows via drone.

Paul works with one ultra-high-net-worth individual who has a trophy room of fallen drones that Paul has taken out for him. Paul chuckled. This international celebrity has fourteen drones that paparazzi have sent to take pictures, and that Paul's shield defence system has taken out.

'One issue is that the drone defence system takes out any Wi-Fi in the whole neighbourhood, as well as ATMs, traffic lights and doorbells. This is only for the duration of you pressing the button but it's sobering to think of this power and what could happen if these military grade jammers fall into the wrong hands.'

All of the close protection officers that we met at John's conference are there to protect and preserve the life of their principals. Just think about what happens when close protection is taken away from a VIP. One of the best examples of this was the late Princess Diana. As a working royal, she had full royal protection from specialist, highly-trained armed police officers, a wealth of real-life David Budds.

However, by the time she died so tragically in the tunnel in Paris, she had lost her right to royal CP so was left unprotected in a car that was not safe. She was not wearing a seatbelt and was with a driver who was over the legal limit. She was unprotected, vulnerable and she paid the highest price. If Princess Diana had had full royal protection that night in Paris she simply wouldn't have died. She would have been safely belted up in the back of an armoured car driven by a specialist skilled driver, in a convoy of vehicles with multiple armed CP officers. It just shows what can happen when the sophisticated close protection operation around an individual is removed, and how complex and multi-layered a top-level CP operation needs to be.

We met John again in the summer of 2022 to discover what he has learned from all these years in the public and private sector. John emphasised the need for both soft and hard skills in non-hostile environments and the importance of building a rapport with the principal. He described it as 'a fine art'. A lot of ex-military guys, he said 'don't fit so well in Harrods or in the front seat of an S500 Mercedes. Whereas someone who has the chat and the charisma to fit nicely into an entourage can go far. I used to be a close protection trainer and I would bring them back from Afghanistan and put them into Harrods and tell these guys, "You can do this! You just have to understand how the ultra-high-net-worth individual lives.'"

John has a lot of time for ex-special forces guys. He does say, though, that some of them still have an itch to scratch and desperately want to get back to the front line, finding it frustrating travelling around Mayfair and catching private jets to Monaco. Often these guys ride motorbikes and sports cars. They need the adrenaline rush and looking after someone's fifteen-year-old daughter in Center Parcs doesn't quite cut it.

We asked John about his impressions of the super-rich. What had he learned from all this proximity to people with bottomless wealth and privilege?

He thought and smiled. 'I've flown to the Cayman Islands and been on superyachts after being up close to extreme poverty. How do I psychologically deal with it? How do I de-escalate? It is a difficult one.'

There's the inevitable personal toll too. 'I tell these guys: "yes, you are going to be on a private jet in Sardinia, but you are going to miss your kid's first birthday." You have made that decision. Our industry is fast personal deployments. It's the job.'

We pressed him on the super-rich. 'The type of people

who make this kind of money have brains that operate continually. They are busy people who love to be busy and are never not busy. They can never stop working. If I was them I would think, I am missing my kids growing up here. Stop. You don't need any more money. Stop. Enjoy your life with all the money that you have. Money is not everything and I have seen it. It helps, obviously, but beyond a certain point it is meaningless.'

John shared a memory of being in the car with a fifteen-year-old Middle Eastern client. The boy said, 'John, I want to go to Harrods and buy the biggest and most expensive cuddly toy they sell for my sister', to which John said, 'No, let's go onto Moonpig and let's get personalised pictures of you both and write a really special letter.'

We asked him if the boy took this advice.

'No, we went to Harrods and he spent 700 quid on a cuddly toy.'

## Chapter 18

# LOCKDOWN

For the whole world in 2020, even pampered, cocooned super-rich like John's young client, there was no event bigger than the global pandemic. It had multiple, complex implications for both our contributors and the universe of close protection.

On the evening of Monday, 23 March 2020 the then Prime Minister Boris Johnson announced a total lockdown across the United Kingdom to slow down the spread of the killer virus COVID-19.

Just days before the unprecedented lockdown, Jonathan had driven up for another visit to Sarah Johnson at the Northamptonshire Police headquarters. Sarah had been chosen to run the whole force response to COVID-19.

The atmosphere in the station was understandably tense as the scale of the crisis began to emerge. Replicating the emerging pattern all over the country, many officers were themselves falling ill with suspected cases of the virus, creating a resourcing issue at a time when the force was most needed. They not only had to sign off if they were ill themselves, but also because of the Public Health England guideline to do so if someone in their household displayed symptoms – fourteen days of self-isolation was required.

Reports were coming in of the looting of chemists for paracetamol. Supermarket trollies were pushed out of stores heaving with food, followed by a distraction technique and a dash outside to steal the goods. Scammers were going house to house stealing money from vulnerable pensioners. There was rising panic in the community. Sarah was managing uncertainty amongst officers, facing a situation like no other, and worried for their own families and their ability to carry out their duty if they fell ill.

Sarah's crisp update to Jonathan conveyed the incredibly dynamic nature of the situation since he had last seen her running the Prince Harry close protection operation.

'We have gone from 0–60 in that containment phase really fast. We closed an entire station at one point. We lost a whole night shift of officers who had been in touch with an infected person. An officer had been caring for her brother and father who had been in Italy and both confirmed positive with COVID-19. We had to shut the station as she almost certainly had it. We also had an awkward incident where someone drove a lorry of clandestine migrants into custody. We opened it up and found out they were all from Iran, which is a Level 1 country for COVID-19. We have had some real challenges. The key workers definitions came out, now the schools are shut, we are responding day to day to big changes as they are announced.'

Sarah rolled her eyes and laughed, looking at her second-in-command, Elliot Foskett.[Elliot is now Assistant Chief Constable at North Yorkshire Police]'We are pulling twelve-hour shifts now every day. What did you do before, three hours a day?'

'Oh shut up,' Elliot retorted.

'Elliot used to be a sailor.' Sarah smiles. 'And you know what his official title was in the navy? Bunting tosser!'

Another officer, Mark, who had joined the Covid team, entered the conversation at this point. They had recalled many officers from secondment, and it was all hands on deck.

Mark was trying to calculate how many officers they had already lost. How many were at home sick, how many were self-isolating because of family members. News broke that the chief constable of Staffordshire had the virus. Prince Charles had contracted it. Boris Johnson ended up in intensive care because of it. No one was immune, even at the highest echelons of British society.

Sarah called her team over. 'Lockdown is coming, it is the next stage. We need an operational lead for lockdown and I want to suggest Sarah Louise Parrot. She has community response, military background and public order experience. She is going to build a deployment plan linked to public order, research on quarantine legislation and to look at how we are going to provide food and drink to officers in a time of lockdown when nothing is open. What does our deployment structure look like? How do we link that to incident response? Do we have enough PPE? We think this is the next big bit of work to be done. This is going to reach across response, crime. We haven't done lockdown since the Blitz and we need to work out what that looks like.'

Sarah and her team had a conversation about European crime trends during the pandemic. What they could learn from countries unfortunate enough to be ahead on the disease curve, particularly Spain and Italy, to get a sense of what was likely to happen in the UK.

Sarah turned to Jonathan, her tone grave. 'It's a race each day now. We are building three teams, a superintendent, an inspector plus a staff officer to run each team 24/7 over the coming weeks. We have a regional conference call this morning to see what other forces are doing in terms of teams and officers.

'I don't know how quarantine legislation has been applied in other countries and how it applies to us. I know that Israel have relaxed all their surveillance monitoring powers. However, here it needs to be done with compassion and with the values of the service. These aren't criminals, people are frightened.'

Another officer entered and Sarah explained the plan constructed around Teapot 1.

'The Met run Teapot 1. It is run by retired officers and they turn up with food and drink, and with the lack of canteen function we are very likely to need something similar. It is to be run by ex-officers and volunteers.'

Next, a major conference call came to discuss force responses to the crisis. On the phone were police leads from Lincolnshire, Derbyshire, Leicestershire and Nottinghamshire.

Derbyshire had 64 self-isolating officers a few days ago and it was now 362. Lincolnshire had gone from 9 to 39. All over the region officers were down. This information could not be revealed to the public for obvious operational reasons. No one wants criminals to feel that they are operating in an environment with a lower risk of being caught.

Talk turned to the role of the military during a lockdown. What would they do in terms of back-filling in the case of mass casualties?

The tone of the conversation was brisk and business-like, despite the extreme nature of the topics under discussion. The forces compared the new issues they were facing. 'We have had issues in supermarkets where people are dashing out with a load of trolleys.'

Talk turned to the official guidance around what constitutes a 'key worker'. It was still somewhat ambiguous, no one seemed to know whether it applied to both parents or just one in terms of being offered childcare provision in schools or nurseries. The British government appeared to have left it deliberately opaque and open to interpretation.

Sarah entered a Gold meeting with the chief and representatives from across the force. She had to do a significant presentation on the whole situation. It went through what all the Bronze commanders were doing across the force in this extremely fast-moving scenario.

'We get a number of pieces of information from a number of different sources. Not just central government, not just COBRA, but also the national police chiefs' council, the college of policing and many other sources. Our chief is passionate about delivering to the public and delivering to the teams. We talked about Teapot 1 and that went down well. Blitz British feeling. We talked about the issue of working from home in the force. We aren't really set up for that, police don't really work from home, it's not that sort of job.'

As the only Silver commander in the force dealing with COVID-19, there was a great deal of personal pressure on Sarah. Fortunately she found Elliot to be a great support. 'You were so calm, so measured, it's the "swan effect", there was no question that you couldn't answer and you hit the right tone completely.'

At this very early stage, Sarah predicted that it would take six months before things calmed down.

'It feels like World War Z at the moment. There is real dynamism. Elliot described it as like running a homicide, didn't you? You get new information every day and you spin that wheel every day and look at the new information as it comes in. Every time the government announce something new we have to react and change and come up with a structure around it. Things will level out. However, I think this critical phase of the virus will last six months and I don't anticipate doing anything but this for the next six months. After that point we will either have another resurgence or we will start to let things relax a little and manage the virus.'

Sarah compared dealing with coronavirus to what she normally does in firearms. 'I like a firearms job, there are difficult challenges, but this is completely different. One thing you have to realise is that we are working to Public Health England on this, it is a health emergency and while it impacts us we don't own it. This is really weird for the police, as when there is a terrorist attack we are used to leading it, owning it, commanding it. It's not the case on this one. We are subject to their advice and guidance on all of our staff. However I don't think I'll be involved in anything else like this in my career. It is fascinating. To problem-solve some of these strange and unique things that are coming through? We have never had any of this stuff to look at before.'

We discussed the edict that ISIS recently put out telling its global supporters not to go to Europe because it is too dangerous. That this is the only war in history that we can fight by sitting on the sofa and watching Netflix. We had a lighter moment regarding the rumours in Northampton the night before that there would be army on the streets of the town guarding and rationing loo roll.

They could, of course, anticipate changes to crime during this period. As Elliot said: 'I am not going to lie, three months of martial law and quarantine will do wonders for our crime stats.'

Sarah caveated though, that crime might simply alter rather than reduce. 'What is interesting is how crime will just change during this period, we will see a lot more scamming, a lot more child sexual abuse and images of child sex abuse, more domestic violence.'

Elliot captured her perfectly in a moment when she had stepped out of the room. 'I always thought with Sarah that if I am not calling her Ma'am within a short space of time something has gone seriously wrong. You sometimes spot these people in your career and in your life where you think you are operating at a level unlike anyone else. She's got such a good value set, vision, so knowledgeable and fair, and she is far better than I am at being politically astute and knowing which battles to pick. She is top class.'

Sarah returned and gave her own thoughts on Elliot. 'When I met Elliot he had been working in CID and had got really unfit. We went to a coffee shop together and he was huffing and puffing from just walking there. Me, a passionate boxer, I said come to boxing, you'll love boxing.

Eventually I coerced him into it and although he was sick the first session he persevered with it. We were sparring and Elliot was goading me a little bit and said I hit like a girl.'

Elliot interjects: 'So she hit me in my chest and I thought I was having a heart attack and I sank down and I remember saying if your face is the last one I see before going to my grave I'm going to be furious! I tried to box on but it was so, so painful, so I went to A&E. The nurse was like, what's your name and went through the details and asked me what happened. She went down a list of things and said, "I'm sorry, there is nothing on my list that says anything about being punched whilst having a midlife crisis, have you tried Zumba?"'

They both laughed heartily. On a less humorous note, Elliot was out of action for six weeks and had several broken ribs. They have been firm friends ever since.

Coronavirus did not stop the criminal world turning. With firearms jobs throughout the lockdowns; they were called to murders and attempted murders, and, of course, drug dealing continued through the lockdowns.

The virus progressed, and the death toll in the UK overtook that of countries such as Spain and Italy that we had been encouraged to pity as cautionary tales early on, becoming per capita the highest in Europe, and for a time, the world. It became clear that many of the predictions shared with us during that day at Northamptonshire Police were bang on.

As the first UK lockdown dragged on, inevitably civil unrest and mental health issues began to emerge as features for the armed police to deal with. Exactly a month in, on the evening of 23 April 2020, armed police were called to an incident in Chichester after a fifty-two-year-old man was seen brandishing a knife. Following a three-hour stand-off, in which the man was threatening to harm himself rather than others, he surrendered the knife and no deadly force was required. He was subsequently sectioned under the Mental Health Act.

It was, however, the second such incident that firearms officers and negotiators from Sussex Police had been called to in less than a *week*. The armed police had shown themselves to be more vigorous in other nations under lockdown, including China, France, Spain, Italy and the USA. Unprecedented global lockdowns also presented unprecedented decisions in terms of the use of force and deployment of armed police on the streets to enforce emergency pandemic measures.

## Chapter 19

# THE TRAINING

'Trainees spend three days learning how to fire a weapon...and the rest of the course learning when not to pull the trigger.'

All police bodyguards are armed officers first. The close protection course is then open to established and experienced firearms officers as a new and separate course. Some of our non-police bodyguards have taken a different route and not been armed police officers, but what unites them is some form of highly rigorous training.

Let's take it back a step though. How do you become an armed officer in the first place?

Regular police officers who wish to become firearms officers have to undergo a rigorous fifteen-week selection procedure. During this, they will have to demonstrate their knowledge of the law, their appropriate and proportional use of force, their communication skills and common sense. If successful in the application stage they will then go on to an assessment stage where their skills, temperament and fitness will be evaluated. If they pass this phase they will then begin the IFC course that will teach them weapon-handling skills, shooting, advanced first aid and tactics.

Sarah Johnson had one or two other female AFOs over the four forces but otherwise she was the only woman. Her first experience of the training was that it was heavily weighted towards male performance strengths.

'The way we have recruited AFOs over the years is that we say we need people who can make decisions, who are good at teamwork, and then the way we test whether someone is good at teamwork is to carry a log as a team, so it's about body strength. When it comes to decision-making, decide how you can lift this very heavy object.

'There is a ridiculous test called "The long stand" when you are told to stand yourself in front of a door and hold your arm ready, a threat will present itself. But nothing presents itself, they just make you stand there for forty-five minutes. If you do not have upper body strength you will fail that test. And they weighted it so that if you failed your interview and diversity questions you could still pass if you could shoot really well. How is this right?'

Sarah has been changing everything and from our meetings with her it became abundantly clear that it needed changing. The case of serving armed police officer Wayne Couzens using his badge to abduct, rape and murder Sarah Everard shocked and sickened the entire nation, not just the crime itself but the horrific abuse of the trust that the public have in the police.

It emerged that many other officers had some degree of awareness of Couzens' history of flashing and sexual assault. Sarah Johnson is at the forefront, from training onwards, of trying to change a deeply embedded culture of misogyny and the 'boys' club'.

In a nutshell, Sarah stopped it being about being able to shoot and made it about being able to learn to shoot; she stopped testing people purely on strength. She introduced alternative memory tests in the place of reciting your top-ten favourite rugby players.

'Before what we were getting was white ex-military men and nothing else came out of the other end of it. One of the problems is that women still deselect themselves from firearms. Culturally we still bring women up to like kittens and puppies and be caring, so they tend to go into domestic violence policing.'

Sarah, though, was really trying to change things. 'Before whereas you might be asked to recount a time when you did something mega and smashed it, I asked them to tell me about a time when they last failed and how they recovered from it. I asked them to tell me about what you do when you make a mistake. So many of them failed it and I got some proper shit over it. I was told that I wasn't selecting proper firearms officers, that there was a type, but I just pushed on. And my department now looks more like *The Inbetweeners* and less like *The A-Team*. Which for me is a massive benefit. It's culturally diluted, we have more difference, we have language skills, they are younger and they look different and sound different. It's great!'

Sarah applied this change across the four forces. When the collaboration ended, her force and one other stuck with it and the other two ditched her ideas and went back to the old way. Most chief officers understood it as Sarah intended, as a change and as a progression. It was recognised nationally and Sarah stands by the ideas and the changes. Nearly every force in the country turned up when she presented the ideas to change firearms recruitment.

Sarah does not want to stop with firearms. She wants to change the whole service, including the senior officers who she describes as overwhelmingly 'white men over a certain age. What do they know about my desire to have weird tattoos or strange likings of Harry Potter? There is no diversity in the senior officers really.'

Sarah's talent, commitment and innovation has ensured that she has moved swiftly up the ranks. In her typically enthusiastic view of her amazing police career, 'Even the boring bits are interesting. I've been on a firearms commanders' course. Gold/Silver/Bronze. I passed my strategic firearms course. I get updates on what is happening in the firearms world. Formative and summative teaching tests you.'

Now, she wants to do the counter-terrorism training. The pandemic and the widespread protests tested Sarah and the entire police force too. Sarah was there to provide police support at both the Black Lives Matter protests and Extinction Rebellion. The latter took place throughout Covid, which the media didn't report.

Sarah says: 'I consider myself to be a liberal person. In my entire service I have only come across one officer I would describe as racist – my tutor – he said racist things, and left shortly afterwards.'

The police reflect the public. Sarah finds it concerning that the police service are the only service considered for their racism. 'Why are other services not considered? Some of the things I've heard people say to me as a police officer appal me. "I'm going to whip out your spine and beat you to death with it." I prefer an innovative insult!'

So how did she end up in firearms, we wanted to know? Back at work after a period of maternity leave, Sarah encountered a 'bit of a hoo-ha'. One of their officers had gone into the firearms range with a dog handler. They thought it would be funny to strip down to their pants and put it on Twitter. It caused a massive incident. The chief came down and said: 'This department needs a massive shake-up, it is too macho, I don't like it' and, almost overnight, Sarah got made head of firearms.

Sarah says: 'It was very tokenistic if you think about it. It was like, "there's a bird, she wasn't involved, let's put a woman in charge." Suddenly I am head of the firearms department. I was a very experienced firearms commander by this point. I am in this job in charge of the training, the governance, the management. I get given this department and I was like, "yes, I have got my dream job." About eight months in, they say "Let's do a regional collaboration with four other regions."'

This was a massive change, involving Northamptonshire, Lincolnshire, Leicestershire and Nottinghamshire. 'All thrust together to find a way to put together probably the most culturally testy area of the service into one. They split the four forces into a north and a south.'

Sarah was the only female in the whole collaboration and it emerged that one role that was coming out of this new collaboration was a new role called Specialist Firearms Inspector.

'They are going to have a team called The Tactical Armed Policing Team who are going to be proactive, basically a group of ninjas who are going to do a range of pre-planned jobs. They are all SFOs, specialist firearms officers who can swing through windows in balaclavas, the MAST [mobile armed support to surveillance team] jobs, all the exciting stuff.'

Sarah got the job. She was doing counter-terrorist related jobs and lots of MASTS where they follow and strike.

Sarah says she can't make women sign up. However 'there are a lot of women who just don't want to hold a gun.' The other side of that is that Sarah says there are now lots of old-fashioned male recruits who no longer want to sign up to firearms. 'We have made it too fluffy apparently.'

She smiled when Jonathan referenced the 50 per cent fail rate nationally on the firearms fifteen-week course.

'You know where that comes from, don't you? That we have designed such a hard course that half the people have to fail it. It is intentional. It is about men applying it to other men and them saying, "Do you look like an AFO, do you sound like an AFO? We are the best, we are elite." Screaming at officers on the range. It's not the military but there was a military attitude pervading through. Our pass rate in Northamptonshire is nearly 90 per cent as we don't find strangeness or difference unacceptable. The idea that there is only one way to do firearms? Not helpful.'

Whether it's the newly devised course led by Sarah Johnson or the more old-fashioned firearms training course, undoubtedly the training is extremely hard.

Those high-calibre individuals who pass the course and assessment to become AFOs are then regularly tested on fitness and tactics and are required to pass qualification shooting to remain in permit. Following competence in the role of an AFO, further courses and development are available to officers to progress. Some officers provide an armed response capability to police surveillance teams (MAST) and Chemical, Biological, Radioactive, Nuclear Firearms Team (CBRN). Others provide armed protection to members of the royal family, government officials and visiting heads of state. As we have seen, Sarah's husband Chris, for example, is trained as an armed protection officer for the royals.

Some examples of the different kind of Police Firearms Officers include:

- Specialist Firearms Officer (SFO)
- Counter-Terrorist Specialist Firearms Officer (CTSFO)
- Armed Response Vehicle Officer (ARVO)
- Tactical Support Officer (TST)
- Close Protection Officer (CPO) & Personal Protection Officer (PPO)
- Authorised Firearms Officer (AFO)

Husband Chris's training had similarities to Sarah's but there were differences too.

Chris described many quirks of the training. 'For example, "the big red hammer": you smash the door in and go in, then you use disk cutters to go through certain doors. There is a bunker, it is a corridor with rooms off it. You go through doing your drills using everyday policing objects.

'They show you a submission guide then as a test you go into a bunker, and you had to strip it and reassemble it.

They put you into everyday policing matters. They are after a good all-round police officer they can train to be a firearms officer. You have to train with a respirator too.

'Then my interview was a bit of a car crash, but luckily I scraped through. I remember turning up on the first day of my course. They said the interview was appalling but I did so well on the other aspects…'

This was September 2005 and he had to wait to go up because he'd done so badly at interview. As a firearms officer you have to train every six weeks. You have to pass shooting tests: three days of training every six weeks. Chris was sent on an advanced driving course too. It was a four-week course with a more powerful car. He passed that and went straight on to his team.

As Chris explained: 'The book doesn't always reflect "real life". You have a mentor to see you through that transition. There's a national decision model, a way of making you think about what is in front of you. Do we have the legal powers to do this? We have working strategies, kind of like "what ifs?" You build up a thought process.'

Because of this excellent training, 'British police officers, the way we resolve threat and risk incidents, we resolve them really well. To become a close protection officer you have to be an AFO. Those posts are really contested.'

Today, every UK police constabulary maintains a specialist firearms capability. It contains tactical team members trained to AFO standard or higher. With the exceptional training that they are given, AFOs carry out law-enforcement operations far beyond the capability of standard unarmed police officers.

# Chapter 20

# CHRIS AND SARAH

'My career has been amazing but it's a love/hate
relationship.'

Typically self-deprecating when we interviewed him,
claiming that his wife Sarah has a much better memory,
Chris Johnson kindly took us through how two decades had
shaped him as a close protection officer.

When he was quite young at school, he did the cadets
course, and that led to an interest in joining the armed forces
or police. He went through military selection for the Royal
Marines but got injured. He was planning to give it another
go. Instead he worked at Tesco.

Then Chris met a special constable and joined the
special consta-bulary [the UK's network of volunteer police
officers]. His interest in the military declined, and his first

taste of the constabulary cemented his desiren to be in the police.' He did specials in Northants for two and a half years. There he could see a glimpse to transition from special to regular. He applied for Northants police in early 1998 and failed the selection process. The regulars said: 'Go to the Met, they take anyone!' But he snapped a ligament, and the Met rejected him on medical grounds. This delayed him by six months but then he got in and did four years in the Met.

Northants was a fairly rural beat but in the Met he got posted to Barking and Dagenham. He had lived in a village and been to private school. When he joined in late 1998 at age twenty-two, his mum was still looking after him.

'Barking & Dagenham, where's that?' You had a tutor constable at Barking station to take you through the basics.'

He started out stopping people at traffic lights. With one guy, Chris looked over the form and the first box is sex: 'Is it Mr?'

'Are you taking the fucking piss?'

Chris said, 'You could be a doctor or a professor.'

The guy got his ticket and was aggressive. 'There was an unpleasant estate in Barking called the Gascoigne Estate. They would throw tins of paint coming out of flats, a colleague had a fridge freezer thrown at him. Another guy gave the 30th of February 1970 as his date of birth!'

Chris told us that 'Once a colleague kicked the door down and a guy jumped out of the window and impaled himself on railings. In the "canteen culture" that existed then that officer got ripped for months. There was an unpleasant tone in some cases, like picking on female officers. At other times, banter makes it tolerable though. Humour is a coping strategy, but was also frowned upon to a certain extent.'

In terms of Trauma Risk Incident Management (TRiM), the police force is very good now at wellbeing. They are putting things in place to help people, but if police officers see something particularly horrific, they want to be with their mates. Things are changing, there is less bottling up now, you can show your emotional side.

'They say, "We are big rufty-tufty firearms officers, we can't show emotion." I worry about me, am I going to have a wellbeing issue? But back in 1998, it was very much a case of "man up". You have to do nasty stuff, but then you had canteen culture, still a bit of having to put on a brave face. Some people do bottle things up.'

Chris struggles to come home and talk to Sarah about some things, but Sarah can pick up on an issue. You might be dealing with a horrific road traffic accident where someone has died. Then within seconds you have to switch to dealing with someone threatening someone with a firearm across town.

Back to 1998… Chris rented 'a horrific flat, I didn't get on with my flat mate, I kept going home, then I moved home and got my head snapped off!'

In the latter part of 2002 he had his old bedroom back from his mum and dad, £250 a month all in. He had disposable income, a nice car. When he met Sarah he didn't have a penny, though. He had spent it all!

Working the beat in Northampton, Chris horribly injured his wrist. He stopped a driver who ran off, the guy barged past him, he rugby tackled him and he fell to the ground. The doctor said it was just a sprain. Eighteen months later, he still couldn't pick up a kettle or shake hands. It was a broken bone, but by then it was too late to do anything. This was seventeen years ago, and Chris is still bitter about the whole thing. It was one broken bone, now three broken bones, the first broken bone became arthritic. It's called Kienböck's disease.

His surgeon said the best thing to do is a wrist fusion. It's his right hand and he's right-handed; he has even googled wrist replacements. Sarah says his movement has been different for years.

'I'm fine when I'm shooting a pistol, but going for the gun in a holster on my belt is another story.'

His memory of work isn't always that good. Chris doesn't know if that is to mask past trauma. Domestic incidents are a big part of what firearms officers deal with. Some firearms jobs can be mundane.

'We would always err on the side of caution. The threshold to pull the trigger is painfully high. I've been doing some work around knife crime and gun crime: 1600 Taser incidents last year, out of that 1600, 1 per cent of Tasers were actually fired. The red dots on a chest make people pause.

You can *aim* it and fire it up and that's usually enough to subdue people.'

Sarah wanted to talk about the difficulties of them both being in the police. There were so many difficult conflicts. One cop told them to bring their baby in and have it in a cot in the control room all night!

'Chris's mum is just down the road and she gets called sometimes. That handover in backyards of police stations… A case of needs must. My career has been amazing but it's a love/hate relationship. When it's good, it's great. I find it difficult with the dislike of the police in the media.'

Chris does practical CP training too, so he's an expert in building the perfect close protection officer. Close protection is a unique set of skills. When you pass firearms training you can go different routes:

- Dynamic intervention (aggressive tactic)
- Rifle training
- Close protection

Chris explained: 'The close protection world is very different, it's a very discreet skill and you need soft skills for the close protection world. You have to be *flexible* in close protection training, which tries to throw dilemmas at you, for example, the car breaks down. It seems simple, but with the principal in the car how do you deal with that? Do you have an advance car ahead of you? A back up car behind?'

Some principals are more switched on than others.

Beneath the surface, there is *loads* of work going on, but on the surface it is very smooth and serene: the swan metaphor.

In training Sarah has experience of pretending to be the principal. She was asked to be awkward, like going to the toilet all the time, like she had cystitis! You must make sure the principal has not left *anything* behind. You are preventing physical harm but also protecting their image, for example if someone left a briefcase somewhere.

When Sarah spent a day acting as a principal she went around a university. They lobbed a cup of sugar over her and that was it, she was 'sugar tits' for the rest of the day. They whisked her out. Then she was awkward again back at her hotel and checked into the gym. You can plan and plan, but awkward things occur. Training is invariably more awkward. 'Dilemmas' are what they term the car breaking down or the unexpected gym visit. Sarah explained further.

'You have to have a rapport, a relationship with your principal. You have to build a working relationship or they ignore you and won't tell you their plans. You have to have good social skills. You can form a conversation at a party with anybody from builders to very high-profile people. On jobs I have run we are adamant that it is a low-profile response. We are quite a small force, we have to make sure we have resilience.'

Sarah Johnson provided incredible access for us, allowing us to go out with her on entire shifts and let us see exactly what it is like to walk in her shoes. She is a credit to us all, the embodiment of selfless public service and a tremendous role model, often sacrificing her health, family time, sleep and general wellbeing to protect us all.

Jonathan visited Wootton Hall, the Northampton Police headquarters, on 28 January 2020 to meet Sarah for the first time. They sat in the canteen with tea and talked about how she manages having three small kids with her job. Sarah was tall, with a spiky stylish haircut. She was muscular and fit looking with big engaging eyes and a huge smile. She introduced Chris, who would also be so important to this book, in the following manner.

'My husband is a firearms officer in my department. This morning he has literally finished his night shift, we have done a hot handover of the children on the doorstep. He comes in at 7 a.m., will sleep for an hour then will do the school run and I am in work just after seven. We have been doing this for twelve years with children now, fourteen years altogether.'

Sarah knew she wanted to be a police officer aged twelve, but it wasn't a path her parents wanted her to follow. Her parents were lawyers, she went to private school in Ely, Cambridgeshire and the expectation for her was law or medicine. Her brother is a consultant and her sister married a multi-millionaire. Sarah went to university in Guildford to do podiatry and was at that stage very much on the correct path. When she got to the end of her degree she knew that she didn't want to do medicine. Her parents saw it as a period of rebellion but Sarah didn't see it that way. She dreaded a linear career with a linear career path.

'I was with a boyfriend at the time that my parents loathed. We went to a fete in a park and there was a man from the police, all in leathers, handing out leaflets for people who might be interested in joining the police. I thought yeah, let's do this.'

She trained at Bramshill House Police College in Reading.

Sarah came to Northampton after a ten-week long residential course, and went straight into a force. One of the first jobs she attended was to a sex worker called Helen who was well known to the local police. She had been badly beaten up by her pimp and the officer she was assigned to as her 'trainer' wasn't interested. He took the pimp outside, told him not to do it again and gave him a ride home. Sarah reported him after ten days of deliberating. Sarah and her trainer were separated and Sarah was assigned a female officer called Andrea.

'She is awesome... Just to be clear she did get my teeth knocked out one night though. We went to the town centre on a Saturday night and she told me not to chat shit with the drunks of Northamptonshire. It was a really busy night. There was a big fight outside a nightclub where someone had used the poles used to marshal the queue outside a nightclub as a weapon against one of the bouncers.

'We were outside a pub doing an "all you can drink" night.

One guy inside had his nose bitten off in a fight and they made the decision to close the pub. They kicked everybody out. There were only four of us officers there together and we had to shepherd a whole group of them down the street. It took the group about five minutes to realise that we were on our tod and they ran at us. Andrea smashes her chap and he's on the floor.

'I got a tap on the shoulder and I turned around and just got hit in the face and he knocked me out and then kicked me in the face when I was on the floor. I hadn't seen it coming. He was a big lad. He gets arrested and I am stuck in the back of a van and I get taken to the hospital, but because it was so busy they just dumped me out of the van and went back to the town centre. So I am in A&E, bleeding, in uniform on my own with no front teeth and I am so confused and concussed. I couldn't talk because of my teeth and I go up to the desk. I take my name badge off and give it to her and then go and sit in a chair. I was bleeding into my lap for about two minutes and then I was so confused I got up to walk back to the nick.'

Luckily she was spotted. 'The kind older security guards retrieved me from down the road and took me back to the hospital and then Andrea arrived. I am in casualty later on, they think I have popped my jaw, but I am so confused I get it in my head that the man that did it is next door. He's not but I am getting more and more agitated. My inspector, he says, "You have got to give her a painkiller", and it is so cold on these night shifts I have layer after layer and as I peel off each layer I finally get down to a pink G-string with the word "pussy" on it with my inspector standing there. He never said a word. Not in the rest of his entire career.'

She concluded with a smile. 'What Andrea will tell you about that incident is that she broke a nail and no one gave her any sympathy.'

Sarah's enthusiasm for the job, despite her attack and despite her parents' horror at their daughter having her teeth knocked out, is infectious. 'Remember when you were at school and you go on a naughty mission, you are with all your friends. It is the same thing. We are going to his house, you take the front, I am going round the back. You are one team. You laugh so much.

'I remember going to a house with Andrea one night and we go to the front and there is nothing but screaming coming from the house. And we go round the back and there is a gun on the floor. We pick up the gun and try and go to the front to try and force entry. Out of the bushes comes a completely naked man. "Why are you in the garden naked?" we ask. "Well, that's Gary in there," he says, pointing to the house. "I was in there, err, talking to his wife and he's not very happy about it."'

At that point Sarah was unarmed frontline response. 'Billy Basic' as she describes it. Within eighteen months she started thinking about being a sergeant. She passed the exams and got offered an acting post, which she did for eighteen months. Working separately led to the breakdown of her relationship with her then-partner Andrea. When, after two years, Sarah started to study for her inspector's exams, she met who she describes with a smile as 'the lovely Christopher'.

He was a PC on the response team while Sarah was on communities. Chris had transferred from the Met and was already interested in becoming a firearms officer. An opportunity came in for Sarah to do some project work, strategic-based police work. She did this for eighteen months and passed her inspector's exams. Then her mind turned to firearms. The deputy chief constable knocked on her door at this stage and offered her an acting inspector role as a staff officer for the assistant chief constable.

Sarah was being groomed for high office. She moved in with Chris and got engaged, married and pregnant. By this point she was a substantive inspector having passed her board. Chris joined firearms during this period having passed the fifteen-week course.

Originally wanting to join the military, Chris got into Sandhurst but decided at the last minute that it was not for him. Sarah describes Chris as a very good fit for firearms. She herself was in the early stages of pregnancy when she went on a firearms commander course. She got offered the post and became a tactical firearms commander (TFC). This role was to assess spontaneous incidents and decide whether firearms officers should be present, and if they are to attend what they should do and how they will do it, up to and including deciding whether to take a critical shot. This is the role that Cressida Dick had when Jean Charles da Silva e de Menezes was mistakenly shot dead in Stockwell Underground station. It is a role that comes with huge responsibility.

'The only thing that can fail you as a firearms commander is not being able to make a decision.'

Sarah was running 'epic sieges, people being shot in the street. It was my job to run these incidents. In the middle of the night in the police station when you are running the operation you are the highest-ranking officer, so the buck stops with you. There is no one else to ask. You can wake the superintendent up in the middle of the night three ranks higher than you, but you wouldn't do that unless it was very serious.'

Sarah says it turned out to be 'something I am really good at. It suits my brain. I like running simultaneous risks.

'I was deploying Chris my husband regularly at this point. He did get some ribbing about it. We ran a really protracted siege and that did cause some real problems with our kids as Chris was the Bronze and I was the TFC and it was going on for twelve hours and there was no one else to take our roles. My boss was like, "Can you bring the baby in? Can he sleep in one of the rooms?"'

Sarah talked about the vacuum of silence that happens after she gives the command for the firearms officers to move forwards on a job. There is no live bodycam footage like there is in the movies; she is in a control room and blind, waiting to hear what has happened and what the officers have found.

She describes it as a 'pause point', when 'you feel your heart beating in your throat. You don't want people to die. It's hard.'

Sarah did this job until she was full-term and then had her eldest, Charlie, in 2008. She had six months off, believing she would be desperate to get back to work but was amazed by how much she fell in love with Charlie: 'He's amazing, best thing I have ever done by a million miles.'

'Going back to work broke my heart, I felt awful about it. I was working four on and four off and my mum and mother-in-law would take a day each. I would have him the day before my night shift, stay up all day then do a twelve-hour night shift and then somebody would look after him while I slept during the day. I would do another twelve-hour night shift and then I would have to stay awake and look after him the following day as I couldn't ask anyone for more childcare.'

A lot of Chris's friends have stay-at-home wives and he had to come to terms with the fact that he has, according to Sarah, 'one of the most macho jobs in the service and a wife that is both a rank above him and who is having an effect on Chris's duties and it was so hard.'

Who the default primary carer was has switched at different times for Sarah and Chris. Sarah said: 'It was definitely me at the beginning and I had all the responsibility for everything including Chris's calendar. I felt fatigued.'

In January 2011, Sarah left the control room and went into ops. She was in the same general department as her husband.

Sarah's next promotion was to a chief inspector. But not *just* a chief inspector. Sarah was made a detective chief inspector even though she had never been a detective. It was really hard for her. Every bit of her experience so far had been about 'looking at a threat, here are the tactics, let's solve it. Whereas detective work isn't like that.'

Sarah passed, though, and 'shortly after that a temp superintendent post came up and I became head of firearms, head of public order, head of chemical, biological, radioactive and nuclear'. Her career has been nothing short of stellar. She thinks differently too. That's part of why she's charging up the promotional ladder.

By 2021, her department had grown around 50 per cent during the previous eighteen months. It is the jewel in the crown of the force. Sarah was, for example, the face of the tragic Harry Dunn story in Northamptonshire, as the road accident death caused by an American CIA operative's wife took place in her force area.

Sarah says you can't put it back in the box and she hates that about her work. She believes 'Chris will never fully recover from doing this job. He has worked night shifts for twenty years and won't recover from some of the experiences.'

It was an unusual situation for the police. 'I am working with the most experienced officers in the force, I am one of their mate's wives, I am pregnant, young, female and new. And for some of the traditional core group of officers, often ex-military, they weren't keen. It was a very challenging role but I loved it.'

She continues: 'One of the first firearms jobs I had was two men fighting in the street with a gun. We got four calls, then another six calls, all saying there are two men chasing each other in the street and they have a gun. This is on a Sunday morning in a remote village with no police car anywhere near right on the cusp of our area. It turned out to be two Polish men fighting over a starter pistol. They had fallen out and one had threatened the other one with it.'

Often, Sarah explained, people are very keen to focus on one small element of a story. 'For example "a man has turned up at my house with a gun." What he isn't saying is that I am a drug dealer, he is a drug dealer and we have had a falling out over money and I threatened him last week. There is always a bigger story that you find out afterwards.'

Chris was a jobbing AFO at this point and Sarah remembers passing the baby to him and as she left the house she saw his parents coming the other way, arriving to help. Sarah recalls: 'We had some really unpleasant clashes with shifts and duties in this period, it was really, really hard and we weren't sleeping.'

Sarah got pregnant with Wilfred when Charlie was

thirteen months old. When she went back to work as a firearms commander she laughs remembering the senior officers' reaction to her return. 'I went straight back into the control room and it was good. Got my ticket back, they had to check whether you can still do firearms in case your womb might have affected your brain or something. Honestly, what do they think happens to women when they have children?'

'The worst argument me and Chris ever had was in Center Parcs with the boys. We had been up all night and we were exhausted and he said to me, "You can't even look after the kids you have got and you want another one?" It was the most hurtful thing.

'I went away and thought the person that doesn't want the third child wins. I needed to stop. I was causing problems in my marriage and I needed something else to focus on. In February 2012, it was about six months since we had that big argument and it was Valentine's Day and I came down in the morning and Chris had left me a card on the side next to the kettle and in it he had written: "I have had a think, I think you are right, let's have another baby". Monty was born the following year in April 2013.'

We were thrilled to hear the very happy ending of that part of Sarah and Chris's story. It's not surprising, though, that with jobs as high octane and important as theirs, things do not always end so well.

## Chapter 21

# TRAGEDIES AND MISTAKES

What happens after you leave police close protection work? For many, the private sector beckons, where you can deploy your extraordinary skills and training in a new, often lucrative, direction. The risk of mistakes, sometimes deadly ones, is no different in the private sector though.

As we mentioned, Chris sustained a life-altering wrist injury many years ago, but even so he doesn't want to do anything desk-based. In quite a small department, he is worried about going in the control room and working the phone. To avoid mistakes, everything pertaining to firearms is scrutinised and reported. You have to explain the rationale. He is inputting that data.

'Training is very, very particular about the use of force with guns.'

His injury put him on restricted duties. They wanted to use him to make a promotional video for dog handlers. He used to do something called Operation Pacify. It involved working with kids aged between fourteen and sixteen years old and talking about the dangers of knife crime. They asked him to update the presentation as it was ten years old and that's not his forte. He really quite enjoyed it though.

'Kids always ask the question: "Why don't you shoot the gun out of their hand?" We go for the biggest body mass! The key thing is to neutralise the threat. I said that we go for the biggest area. The other officer said we shoot to kill…

'Quite often people will ring and say that there is a man outside with a gun. Once it was a homeless man with a walking stick sticking out of his sleeping bag! We bought the homeless man food from KFC.

'Another job involved kids in a local park chasing each other with guns. We could see it was low-level tactics. It was just kids making a video but somebody saw them. I pointed out that if the police are called out they don't know the guns are fake, and that you might get shot for real!'

We wanted to hear from the close protection officers and bodyguards themselves what happens when things go wrong, and how these situations could possibly have been prevented.

How does a gun get forgotten by an officer on a plane? How did the wannabe assassin ever get as close as he did to

Ronald Reagan, or Princess Anne? In this job, one error or moment of inattention can cost a life.

From Valery's perspective, at government level there are some high-risk scenarios that no bodyguard on this planet can fully protect against.

'Kennedy was a moving target. That was a professional job. Three snipers – and a professional military mercenary fired the fatal shot. You have to do thousands of shots before you can get that shot.'

In Josh's view the response to the notorious assassination attempt on President Ronald Reagan in 1981 was 'very poor, he got very close to the guy with a six shot revolver. How did that happen?' To put it in perspective, Josh described the meticulous planning they go into with a principal, and their heightened awareness of the risks that guarding a political VIP bring.

'We're planning the nearest routes to hospital. I know one old-school guy who wouldn't eat for eight to ten hours before a big job, because if he got shot and needed surgery he wanted anaesthesia. To do it right, you do it properly.'

As Josh went on to explain, armed protection units are always a reaction force. First you get the early team who 'clean the area'. This means a thorough sweep for anyone or anything that look suspicious. Who is that vagrant who looks a bit dodgy? Are there any obstructions to the route? 'Twelve years ago the prime minister was coming into Guildhall. The ramp cylinders are designed to only let one car in.

His car got stuck and badly damaged.' This is the kind of mistake you seek to avoid, as it could put the prime minister in real danger.

This learning process is grounded in some terrible past mistakes and near misses. The modern version of royal protection policy, for example, had its genesis in a kidnap attempt involving the Queen's only daughter, Princess Anne, in 1974. In an audacious attempt, an unemployed manual labourer, Ian Ball, ambushed Princess Anne's car on The Mall.

Taking them entirely by surprise, Ball managed to shoot and injure four men, including the princess's driver. In the end it was passers-by and some more police arriving on the scene who managed to scare him off. It goes without saying that this kind of situation is every bodyguard's nightmare.

Unsurprisingly, this unsettling incident and failure of close protection, which could so easily have ended in tragedy, led to a huge overhaul of royal security, including a major increase in the number of officers who could be used as resources. Although this improved that particular situation, there were many other cases of failings of close protection, some of them truly shocking, that persisted.

Major miscarriages of justice, and even crimes, by close protection officers have been very well-documented. They send shockwaves through the public but even more so through the rest of the police force.

One such event was the shooting of Mark Duggan.

Duggan was a twenty-nine-year-old black man who was shot in the chest and killed by armed officers from the Metropolitan Police in Tottenham on 4 August 2011. Whilst Duggan was under investigation by Operation Trident and known to be in possession of a handgun, the circumstances of his death attracted a great deal of attention and protest.

The police indicated that they were trying to arrest Duggan on suspicion of planning an attack, and officers were cleared by a 2013 Independent Police Complaints Commission (IPCC) investigation, which found no evidence of criminality by the police. The public inquest which ended early the following year also concluded that Duggan's death was a lawful killing. However, conflicting accounts of the events leading up to Duggan's death by the Metropolitan Police attracted suspicion, and outrage at his death sparked riots in London and other major UK cities.

Perhaps the most notorious case of all involving armed officers from the Met was the aforementioned shooting of Jean Charles da Silva e de Menezes, a Brazilian man killed by officers at the London Underground station Stockwell on 22 July 2005. He was a completely innocent civilian who the police wrongly thought to be one of the fugitives involved in a failed bombing attempt the day before. The incident took place just a couple of weeks after the 7 July 2005 London bombings which killed fifty-two people on London's transport network, including the Underground. The shooting prompted mass protests in Brazil and an apology from then Prime Minister Tony Blair, and the debate stepped up about shoot-to-kill policies adopted by the Metropolitan Police since the September 11 attacks.

The manner in which this terrible death was investigated also raised eyebrows. Of the two IPCC investigations, the findings of the first, Stockwell 1, were kept secret and concluded that no officers would face disciplinary charges. Stockwell 2 criticised the police command structure and the manner in which it communicated to the public. In 2006 the Crown Prosecution Service found insufficient evidence to prosecute any named individual police officers, and in December 2008, the inquest returned an open verdict.

For the beleaguered Metropolitan Police, sadly these events do not remain in the past. In Streatham Hill, south London on 5 September 2022, Chris Kaba, a twenty-four-year-old unarmed black man, was shot dead by police during a vehicle stop. His family claimed that it took eleven hours for the police to even notify them of his death. The firearms officer who fired the fatal shot was suspended from duty and the Independent Office for Police Conduct (IOPC) opened a homicide enquiry, but these actions will not bring back Chris Kaba, who was going to become a father and had his whole life ahead of him.

On one occasion we caught up with Chris and Sarah just after the Sarah Everard vigil. They were reeling from the negative coverage of the Met Police during the protests the weekend before on Clapham Common. Decent and committed people, they were torn between their loyalty to the police force and their concern for some of the tactics apparently used.

They had watched the death of George Floyd and ensuing events in the USA with profound unease, too.

Chris's view on George Floyd's murder, and what he said about the contrast with UK police practices was striking: 'It was positional asphyxia: we have been very aware of this for years. It's *not uncommon* for people to say, "I can't breathe, I can't breathe" when multiple police officers are restraining them. We are very aware of it. I can't comprehend why you would kneel across someone's neck. In our training we focus on positional asphyxia. They have Velcro straps they can put around legs and knees… I can't think of any deaths like that of George Floyd in the UK.'

Chris is concerned that when news stories like this break, there is fall-out for British close protection officers. All of the AFOs are very highly trained. This certainly doesn't stop some negativity from the public though.

'A couple of guys at work have had comments. "Why don't you go to America and shoot black people?" I don't think I ever see any racism at work. Racism is not affecting how people deal with situations. If somebody is an arsehole, they're an arsehole.'

Chris has never used a firearm or even had to tase anybody but he has hit somebody over the head with a baton in the line of duty.

'There was a guy running away really fast, then there was a guy with a knife coming at him with a stabbing motion. I drew my baton and batoned him on the head, because he was going to stab and kill that person. He fell in a heap, but he was still holding the knife. It was a domestic incident with his partner. The guy was grateful to me for doing it! He said, "Thank the officer for batoning me on the head because I was going to kill him." I've got no idea what happened to them. Sometimes something about a job just gets into your head.'

Chris and Sarah also know better than most that there are mistakes and errors that don't make the headlines which form a huge part of their job. Not least when they were working together as a couple.

'Sarah was a bit of a shit magnet. Something always went wrong when we were crewed together!'

In one incident, Chris was notified of a 'highly wanted man' housed in a flat. That ended up being a siege for twelve hours. One fellow police officer did not take the job seriously, to the extent that he had booked a hotel room for him and his girlfriend that night. In the end they got negotiators out, who are trained to speak to people. As Chris said, though, 'Negotiators sometimes do more harm than good, because they might turn up after three hours, when the police have formed a rapport. Negotiators go by the book. It doesn't always work that way.'

Some of the worst incidents that Chris has witnessed

have arisen because of the strange dual role played in which firearms officers are also traffic officers. They don't get called out to issue speeding tickets though. They get the complex, dangerous, adrenalin-pumping jobs.

Sometimes it works seamlessly. He had a firearms job on the motorway a while ago. 'You have to try to find ways to stop traffic coming on the motorway.' They managed to do the stop *on* the motorway and it actually worked really well.

As Chris puts it: 'AFOs are interested in dealing with higher-end conflict jobs, not to be out at traffic accidents and catching people speeding. They go to a lot of road traffic collisions. While you are waiting for the ambulance and for your colleagues to turn up, you have responsibility. A fatality is easier to deal with. You:

- Lock the scene down
- 'Call' key witnesses
- Contact the forensic experts

For Chris, the hardest bit is the emotional side. 'Some stuff is *beyond* gruesome. All officers have a different way of dealing with it. But it's the human side. Sad stories. One that sticks in my mind, it was not late at night, it was just a guy renovating his house. He lost control of his car and died. *That's* what gets to me. *That* affects me, not the person trying to stab me or run me over. It can affect police officers in quite a tragic way. It's a *cumulative* effect. It's TRiM: Trauma Risk Incident Management.'

Chris broke down as he described his most traumatic memory of all to Emma. He was in tears describing a house fire caused by some children playing with matches. It was sixteen years ago but it was so horrific he still can't describe it without crying. He saw two children being carried out... went to a trauma counselling session afterwards. Big firemen in tears describing it. The session helped but you never forget something like that.

Going back to that combined role of AFO and traffic officer, Chris had an extraordinary story of a major incident.

There are organised groups that go around the country and steal lorries. These people and operations are high stakes, carefully planned, and they have spotters. Their modus operandi is simple: go into a service station and cut open a wagon on the kerbside. They look inside to see what's worth stealing. Normally, they then just steal the load and drive off.

Not on this occasion. It was a few days before his fortieth birthday, just before Christmas. The police intel department were aware of it and notified Chris. 'Cars are easy to stop. You can put a box around it and bring it to a slow stop. *Lorries* are very difficult to deal with. *Stinger* spikes are what you throw out in front of a car to slow it down.'

It was circa two in the morning when Chris got there to try to stop the lorry. All of a sudden, the lorry stopped in lane three of the motorway. The police could only watch in horror as the occupants jumped out and ran across the southbound carriageway. One got hit by a lorry.

Chris got home about 07.00, 07.30. He phoned Sarah, he broke down and couldn't speak.

'Sarah was brilliant, she couldn't have been better. I went and had a shower, put my shorts and T-shirt on.'

It is etched indelibly in Sarah's memory, too.

'It has not been easy for Chris. Chris had to attend where some men had stolen a whole lorry and then stopped in lane three on the M1 and got out and ran across the carriageway. One of the men had been hit by thirty-six vehicles and there was nothing left of him. All Chris could do was watch him bounce from car to car, lorry to lorry, with most of the drivers oblivious they had even hit him. With the tailback that caused, even early in the morning nobody could get to the scene for about three hours. So Chris was stuck picking up body parts with his hysterical mate next to the roadside of a man they had just watched die.'

For an incident like that, the IOPC need to be contacted. Chris and the fellow AFOs who were with him that night went through the procedure. They had to give their account of it. 'We did get a McDonald's breakfast... You are not allowed to confer. Quite early on it was apparent what had happened, and that we hadn't done anything wrong. People were worried that the investigation could go on for years. You worry about getting hauled over the coals.'

The officers gave an initial account, then a more detailed statement. They got a couple of nights off afterwards because it was so incredibly traumatic. They do that for their welfare but also as a safeguarding from the job perspective. They all sat down and read the IOPC's report. No fingers were pointed at them. They hadn't done anything wrong.

Chris can see there is still room for improvement in the support networks, in this macho and male-dominated world. 'If you've got firearms officers having mental problems, carrying a gun is *not* a good idea. The Police Firearms Officers Association is a charity set up by a former firearms officer. They are really good and really proactive.

'Collision investigation unit on the other hand, they get one welfare chat *a year*. There is a culture that exists – where you don't want to get help in firearms. The support networks are a bit crap.'

You have to protect others from these traumas too. Chris was called out to a fatality. A lad on a scooter had got hit by a car and died. The family turned up. The ambulance had declared him deceased. Sometimes grief-stricken people won't listen and they had some stern words from the police. He had been torn limb from limb and Chris would not let them near this really gruesome scene. His colleagues agreed. 'You don't want people seeing their loved ones like that and you have to protect them.'

Mental health in various forms is a *big* part of what the armed police deal with. Not just their own mental health after traumas like that, but mentally unwell people in the community.

As Chris said with classic understatement: 'It can make

it awkward when you throw alcohol and drugs into the mix. Once we were informed of a high-risk missing person. A car was driving around country lanes, the control room called and said they'd spoken to the guy in the car and he said he would kill himself if they didn't back off, by driving into a tree.' Chris was in an unmarked car so they were able to follow him without being noticed. Eventually he stopped at a red light and he was crying his eyes out. They were able to talk him down and save his life.

A couple of years ago Chris was called to a stolen car driving into their county. The driver of the car took to lane one and accelerated towards them. She drove straight into the back of an HGV. The lorry driver *felt* the impact and stopped. That is very surprising in a big HGV. The car was wedged underneath the lorry. They spoke to her. She said, 'Bog off, I'm not talking to you.' It was only then that the control room told them she was suicidal. The control room could have put a marker on the car to say it contained a suicidal person…

Chris reflected: 'A person who wants to kill themselves isn't thinking rationally. She seemed to be okay injury-wise. Suddenly there were flames at the front of the car. We managed to get the door open. She wrapped her arms around the steering wheel, feet around the pedals. We ran for fire extinguishers. Three or four police officers around the car were punching her to get her to let go, punching her arms and legs to get her to release her grip. We thought we were all going to burn to death saving this girl. Just in time, we loosened her grip and dragged her from the burning car.'

Later on, they got a nice letter from the girl's mum and dad. They said she had got help and turned her life around. It's obvious that this part of the job, saving lives, is something that Chris cherishes. 'Not very often people say well done, but it's nice when it happens. Monday nights are fairly quiet but the others…'

For this kind of incident response, you normally have a close team of seven or eight, all medically and hospital trauma-trained. The senior police officer can bring a bottle of water and food with a company credit card. Part of the training is the medical training. The serious collision investigation unit investigate road traffic accidents, and it is as *forensic* as a murder investigation.

Chris tells us: 'We carry quite comprehensive medical kits in the car. You never know when someone is going to get seriously hurt. Oxygen defibs, tourniquets, tubes up your nose. They have a guide to work through quite a stressful situation. We get positive feedback from paramedics and air ambulances, saying we saved a life. One guy came off his motorbike in a very bad way. His helmet came off, trauma to his head, every time we did chest compressions it was pumping the blood out of his head. He died, but we kept him alive long enough to give his family a chance to say goodbye.'

There are other, more day-to-day pressures too. There

was a US study that an officer in the West Midlands told Jonathan about when he was making the ITV series.' Sixty-one male and thirty-seven female volunteers were randomly chosen from a city with more than one hundred sworn officers. Blood samples, blood pressure readings and other pertinent data were collected from them at a medical clinic, and their shift assignments and overtime hours were confirmed from payroll records. Day shift assignments were considered to be those that started between 4 a.m. and 11.59 a.m.; afternoons, starting between noon and 7.59 p.m.; and midnight shifts beginning between 8 p.m. and 3.59 a.m. The officers, who all worked ten-hour shifts, were categorised according to which shift they most often worked during the five-year period preceding the study.

The study showed that shift work can have a negative effect on your waistline and your cholesterol levels. Midnight shifts and less than six hours' sleep can lead to metabolic syndrome. Overtime on midnight shifts is even more damaging. On late shifts, officers may feel more dependent on restaurants and vending machines that 'point them more toward candy, Cokes, coffee, donuts, and fast foods than toward nutritious meals'.

As much as anything else, the job of a firearms officer is simply exhausting, emotionally and physically. Exhaustion can lead to mistakes, and to serious health issues too. A major American study found that retired firearms officers tend to die about six years sooner than other retired civic public servants. This is a terrible truth, that policing actually endangers those who serve. Some officers are forced to work undesirable hours, due to the 'round-the-clock' nature of law enforcement. It becomes all the more important for those on late shifts to rally their personal defences against the potential assaults on their wellbeing. But as Sarah Johnson says, shift work is not going away.

'Officers need to learn how to adjust to it and come out of it as healthy as possible.'

# Chapter 22

# THE FUTURE

The landscape for close protection changed in 2020 just as everything else did. With Covid a lingering menace, and an increasingly fragmented and volatile world, bodyguards and close protection officers will have to evolve to survive.

Sarah represents one version of a new breed. Demographics are changing slowly but surely, with better representation of females and people of colour, although there is still much further to go down that road.

In the UK, we still have a predominantly unarmed police service, something that is almost unheard of globally. Generally there is a warm feeling towards the British police force, but our society is changing. The rise in domestic terrorist incidents has led to an uptick in public support for more armed police. There are huge regional differences too.

To avoid having a fully armed police service in this

country, and to enable the police to still tackle criminals and terrorists with firearms, it seems obvious that we need to have some of our police officers equipped with firearms. The core British police argument is that, by restricting training to the few, we can achieve a standard that is not replicated anywhere else in the world. Besides, not every officer wants all police to be armed. As one senior officer told Jonathan when he was making his ITV armed police series: 'There are some officers around who I worry about being entrusted with a stick let alone a gun!'

The police receive thousands of calls every year relating to armed crime. These calls have to be answered and this may include sending armed officers to investigate. While filming, Jonathan was once told: 'The fastest way to get the police to respond to a burglary in progress is to say that you think one of them has a gun. They will arrive in minutes!'

This situation is morally ambiguous, to say the least. Perhaps the question is not: should all police carry firearms but should we have *unarmed* police these days?

In our contributor Chris's expert view: 'I don't think all police should be armed, the threat is so small. I've been a firearms officer for sixteen years and I have never shot anyone. I think officers should have a Taser.'

Sarah agrees with Chris. She does not want what she termed 'point and shoot' like the USA. She does not believe that all police should be armed. This is despite enduring a virtually daily barrage of assaults.

'My sons understand that mummy's got a gun at work. I don't think it has really sunk in that much at that age, but there will come a point where it will.'

As far as Sarah is concerned, British police officers are incredible – both on and off duty. 'I'm worried about the use of force and how indiscriminate that could be. It's so exceptional for a police officer to be shot at or ambushed in this country. Taser, though, I would say definitely. It's a brilliant tool, and causes far less damage than if you are batoned.'

Valery interestingly pointed out that plenty of people in the UK have firearms. He informed us that you can pick them up at military shows. The shows sell deactivated weapons which are legal to own, but the parts to reactivate can *easily* be bought online. The weapon can then be reactivated in a matter of minutes. Scary stuff. 'If your client has problems with gang society the bulletproof vest is a must. No muscles on this planet will stop a bullet flying in you.'

The old-fashioned values represented by men like Ivan and Laurie may be on the wane. To Ivan, looking back over his long career, 'it's teamwork. With what they have now for close protection, that's not teamwork.'

Private clients ultimately want discreet protection which enables them to do safely whatever it is that they want to do. With wealth and status comes a sometimes unwelcome amount of visibility. You put your head above the parapet and you don't want it blown off. That's where close protection comes in.

It is human nature that not all global VIPs will accept that the protection they are offered is for their own good. We have had extraordinary tales shared with us. The Indian millionaire who had to be extracted from a mass brawl he started in a nightclub to look big. The banker partying in Tbilisi with local women who had to be thrown over Valery's shoulder in his underwear and forced onto a plane. As Valery explained:

'You're in a different environment and in some ways it is a privilege. For example you get to eat at some of the best restaurants in the world, travel on private aircrafts and superyachts, but you're still working, just in a different setting.'

Writing this book taught us that there are no easy answers. What we do know is that the training, commitment and passion that goes into making a close protection officer, from Sarah 'sending daddy into danger' to the highly trained loyalty of royal protection officers, to bodyguarding VIPs in hostile environments, is second to none.

Given the enormous success of the first series of *Bodyguard*, speculation began almost immediately regarding the possibility of a second series. For various reasons, however, it took far longer for the speculation to coalesce around concrete information.

By August 2022, it had been confirmed that Richard Madden would be returning as Police Sergeant David Budd.

However, at this point production had not yet started, and with no filming already in the can, *Bodyguard 2* would not be hitting the screens before 2024 at the earliest. Part of the first *Bodyguard*'s success in the eyes of writer Jed Mercurio was that it was an original concept.

Mercurio had seemed to hint that, given the success of this formula, he might start season 2 with a new formula and storyline rather than picking up the narrative thread from the close of season 1. In terms of returning cast members, fan favourites included Gina McKee as Commander Anne Sampson, Nina Toussaint-White as DS Louise Rayburn, and Ash Tandon as DCI Deepak Sharma.

Given her memorable and engaging performance as David Budd's estranged wife Vicky, perhaps Sophie Rundle would also be back. The cast rotation that Jed Mercurio's other massive series, *Line of Duty*, performs so adeptly could be deployed for *Bodyguard 2*, bringing in exciting new cast members to shake things up alongside established major players.

Excitement is mounting and we will be looking out for the second series eagerly, along with millions of other fans.

# ACKNOWLEDGEMENTS

Thank you to our brilliant, insightful and patient publisher Ciara Lloyd, and James Hodgkinson at John Blake Publishing, to Justine Taylor, and to the wider team past and present at Bonnier Books UK. Thanks to Nicky Gyopari. Thanks as always to our amazing agents through the project, Martin Redfern, Matt Cole and Diane Banks at Northbank Talent Management, you are superstars.

Thank you also to our three children who have lived with this project for several years now.